Psychic Encounters

CRAIG HAMILTON-PARKER

Copyright © 2014 Craig Hamilton-Parker

All rights reserved.

Previously Titled *The Psychic Casebook – real encounters with the paranormal.*

First published in the UK 1999 by Blandford Cassell plc, Wellington House, 125 Strand London WC2R 0BB

ISBN-13: 978-1500759223
ISBN-10: 1500759228

DEDICATION

This book is dedicated to Sathya Sai Baba,
the omnipresent Indian Avatar who keeps
our egos in check and guides us
to the path of love.

CONTENTS

	Acknowledgments	i
	Introduction	3
1	Getting Started in the Media	5
2	Your Mind Reading Powers	41
3	Déjà vu and Psychic Time Travel	56
4	Horrific Prediction by Edgar Allan Poe	70
5	Amazing Spirit Messages	78
6	Evil Spirits and the Ouija Board	99
7	Dead Celebrities make a Comeback	116
8	Flights into the Spirit World	125
9	Lovers from Past Lives	142
10	Miracles with Sathya Sai Baba	156
11	Are you psychic? FAQ	177
	About the Author	184
	Published Books	185

ACKNOWLEDGMENTS

Our heartfelt thanks to all those people who have courageously shared their stories in these pages. In some instances names have been changed to protect the identity of family members and friends.

If you have questions you need answering about the next life please join us at our online community and spiritual foundation where we are pleased to share our expertise and knowledge.

psychics.co.uk

INTRODUCTION

Do not think of the existence of two entities- this world and the next, here and hereafter. Realise that hereafter is here; this world is interwoven with the next.
- Sathya Sai Baba

Never before in the history of humanity has so much energy been dedicated to fulfilling material ambitions, collecting possessions and seeking ever more luxurious comfort. In the process many people have lost sight of the spiritual part of their lives and feel that life is barren of meaning. In this book I have tried to take you back to the ancient spiritual source and also show you what lies beyond death. I hope it will inspire you to continue your spiritual search for direct insight, inspiration and understanding.

The message that shines through this book is that we need not live in perpetual darkness. Everyone can become attuned to spiritual powers and influences. Everyone has latent powers of ESP, mediumship, clairvoyance and all can attain divine consciousness.

Many of the casebooks you will read are from people who make no claims to having extraordinary paranormal powers. They are ordinary people who, for some unknown reason, have had a spontaneous clairvoyant insight. You will read of people who have glimpsed the future, communicated by telepathy, travelled out of the body, proved that they've lived before, or communicated with the spirit world. In addition you will read of people who have had miraculous experiences and in particular read about the Indian holy man whose miracles are happening right now in the UK, Australia and America.

My sources come from my media work and people I have interviewed during my years as a psychic columnist for the national newspapers and magazines in the UK, Australia, America and South Africa. Some stories have been sent to me via my Internet website. In many cases I've changed names and locations so as to protect the identity of the people involved. You will understand that a haunted house does not sell very well and not everybody is friendly towards people who profess psychic experiences. Amongst my large mailbag I receive the occasional unsigned letter from hell fire 'Christians' and there are many conjurers, cynics and sceptics who still seek to discredit all things paranormal.

There was a time when people such as this made me angry and I have appeared on many a television debate to defend our corner. Frankly, I don't care anymore. There's plenty of scientific evidence to support my claims. You can read these casebooks and make up your own mind. Many of the stories are based upon interviews and letters from my journalistic work and have been checked by editors or corroborated by other journalists. The people who have had the courage to tell their stories in these pages are honest individuals.

The stories have been cemented together with casebooks from my own work as a medium and the work of my psychic wife Jane. I have included the messages from the famous medium Doris Stokes and also testimonials and casebooks from sitters who have had consultation with Jane or myself. In addition, you will read about our life as a psychic family and I've even included a few fun, psychic experiments that you can try for yourself. On the advice of the publishers I have not included the evidence of my mediumistic communications with Princess Diana from sittings with her friends. Also, for reasons of privacy I have not included information about consultations with celebrities who have seen Jane or myself.

I don't claim to have all the answers. I'm not a guru and I can't wave a magic wand and make people's problems disappear. Although I have well-developed mediumistic and psychic abilities I do not claim to be more spiritual than the next person. Like you I am also seeking and will continue to seek for the rest of my life. But this is what life is about, for as we seek so we grow and become. On my way I have discovered various treasures and fellow travellers have shared with me their own experiences about their search. I hope that the psychic casebooks from my files, my wife Jane's files, and from all those who have been prepared to help with this book, will throw a little light into this dark world and help guide the way for those who seek spiritual truth.

1 GETTING STATED IN THE MEDIA

'When we drove our young daughter Kalle to hospital on Easter weekend 1992 we had no idea what horrors were to await us over the next few days. As far as we knew Kalle had nothing more than croup." says her mum Karen Kopec from Bishop's Waltham in Hampshire.

'Kalle had just celebrated her birthday and the bright early morning light reminded me of the time, four years ago, when my husband Stan drove me to the hospital to give birth to her.

'Our gentle mood turned to horror when Kalle began to choke at the hospital. She had epiglottises caused by the hib virus- a similar illness to meningitis- that causes severe swelling in the throat- and her attack was so severe that soon she was on a life support machine with all its intimidating tubes, screens and wires.

'Kalle lay in intensive care for three days. The doctors broke the news to us: our bright little girl would never recover. The machine was keeping her alive and, in the unlikely event that she would ever regain consciousness, she would be little more than a vegetable. The machine needed to be switched off.

'And there was another painful decision to make" says Kalle's dad, Stan, 'Which one of us would hold her as they switched off the life support? We both so much wanted to hold our little girl. Karen had brought her into this world so it seemed right that Karen should hug her tight as she left.'

'As the bleepers, monitors and lights became still I saw the light fade too from our little princess" says Karen "I knew that she had gone and what limply lay before me was not our sweet girl anymore. We knew it was now over and at the same time Stan and I simultaneously heard a clear voice in our heads: "I'm not there now, mummy and daddy, please go home."'

Stan and Karen Kopec were left in a state of shock. Everyone else could express their grief, the house was full of family, friends, and neighbours shedding tears, but the couple were numb with unspoken pain. 'I don't know how we could be so strong' continues Karen 'It almost made me feel guilty and, in some ways, frustrated to have to comfort everyone else.

'Now I look back, I feel that Kalle knew that she was going to die- even before she became ill. The day she first became poorly I saw a competition in a magazine for children to draw their ideal house so I suggested that Kalle occupy herself by drawing one. Kalle was normally a very talented four year old artist yet she produced a strange picture that, in retrospect, may have been a premonition of her future'

Karen showed me the drawing. Kalle had drawn a large, square, white building with a flat roof that looked like a hospital. Outside of this she drew herself playing in the pink and blue flowers which Kalle had said was her now. Through the window on the left was a little girl ill in an iron bed with bars. This was surrounded by boxes with wires- a picture that represented her future in hospital perhaps? To the right was another large window but inside there was nothing. Maybe Kalle was saying, this is me now, this is me in the future, but the last room, her death, she didn't understand so in this she drew nothing.

'Another strange thing was that Kalle believed that at night she was be visited by a man called Michael who she used to talk to in front of me. She loved the music of Michael Jackson and I wondered if this was a fantasy about him. On her headstone we put some of the words from his songs and now if I listen to the words of 'Heal the World' and 'Will you be there?', her favourite songs that she sang before her illness. The words now seem particular poignant as they talk about how beautiful the life is hereafter.'

The first communication that Karen and Stan had from Kalle's spirit came in the form of another drawing. A psychic artist, who had never seen a photograph of Kalle, sent the Kopec's a coloured pencil sketch of how Kalle's spirit looked now. Comparing it to a photograph I could see that there was a striking resemblance- the artist, Mave from Liverpool, had even drawn the small mark on Kalle's cheek.. 'The one thing that the psychic artist had got completely wrong though," says Karen "were the eyes- Kalle had brown eyes not blue ones as the picture showed.'

Prior to her reading with myself Karen had briefly met another medium 'He said that he wanted to tell me something from a little girl on the spirit side' says Karen '"She says that she's got big blue eyes now!"'

Karen and Stan felt that Kalle had been trying to communicate with them in other ways too. 'We used to see spiralling blue lights in our room and at other times smelt a overwhelming scent of flowers and a feeling of warmth when we talked about her- a smell that used to follow us then disappear as quickly as it came.' says Stan. 'After she died our doctor friend in Australia received a phone call saying Kalle had died a few hours earlier, he said he knew something had happened because he had seen her figure stood in his bedroom- he didn't even know that Kalle had been ill.'

It was at a psychic fair at Ocean Village in Southampton, where I was giving Tarot readings, that Karen first came for a sitting with myself. 'We only went along because it was raining and we had nothing better to do' says Karen 'little did I know that it would be a life changing experience.'

'Craig lay out the tarot cards but soon pushed them aside saying that he wanted, with my permission, to work with me mediumistically. Although he was tired and the noisy conditions were difficult to work with, there was a lady and a little girl insisting that they talk with me. The lady he described was my aunt who Craig said was helping with the communication. "Your little girl is worried about your mum" said Craig "she's taken her granddaughter's death very badly"- which was quite true. When I spoke to mum immediately after the reading I realised that her depression over Kalle was far, far more serious than I had realised.

'Craig proceeded to give me proof of Kalle's survival of death. He said that she died when she was four but would be six now and that she died covered in tubes and wires in intensive care on the 23rd April. She had, he said, a swollen throat, a bad stomach and passed over just after her birthday of the 23rd March. (her birthday was the 22nd March).

'I was stunned as Craig reeled off the facts about Kalle's passing. He said that her name sounds something like Sally but it was the little things that clinched it. A reading that was supposed to be ten minutes went on for an hour. This was the first time I had got a really positive link with my child and Kalle wasn't going to let Craig go. Tears were running down Craig's cheeks as he made this emotional link.

'Craig described her long brown hair that I had stroked as Kalle lay dying, her favourite red wellies. He talked about her treasured hat with a flower in the middle, her toy helicopter, her racing car with only three wheels, her allergy to cheese and the old teddy, that used to have a red bow, and which had been put in the coffin with her. There was a little pink teddy with her too communicated Kalle- one that her friend gave her at the hospital.

Kalle sent her love to her dad and the my 'dead' aunt interjected to say to stop worrying about the tax bill. Craig said she was talking about Nana Nana with the bad legs and how she lived next door to the pigs. (Nana, Nana was her pet name for Karen's Grandma who I found out later had recently started suffering from her legs) Kalle also expressed her love for her baby brother Luca and said that a new baby brother who looked just like her. He had just been born and she said that there was a little baby sister to come in the near future.

'Craig said that Kalle was showing him an unfinished dolls house that her Dad had made with its pretty pink furniture and how her brother Stefan likes to now play with her toys particularly her helicopter. He described a horse in the mud- a horse had stood on her foot but the soft mud had prevented any bones being broken.'

"Kalle went on to say how she loved her brother Luca and her baby brother Stefan. And she said she would soon have a new baby sister.

"I thought there was no way that could be true. I had been told that I should not have any more children, even though I was desperate to have another little girl."

Karen had already had two Caesareans, while an ectopic pregnancy had left her with extensive scarring. A consultant had said another pregnancy would be very risky, as Karen's womb might not be able to hold the baby.

By the time Stan appeared, Karen was in pieces. "He wondered what had been going on, but I said that I'd tell him when we got home," she says. When they2 talked later both found it hard to come to terms with what had happened. But, during another session with me, I told Karen that she was pregnant with a baby girl.

Although Karen felt this could not possibly be true, she nevertheless found comfort in the sessions. "They gave us strength because, for the first time, we felt as if Kalle was still with us. Her death nearly ripped the family apart; now we felt we could carry on."

But soon after, to her great joy, Karen found out she *was* pregnant- and a scan confirmed it was a girl. The astounded family eagerly awaited the birth of a very special baby.

Kodie was born in November 95 "This is a dream come true," says Karen. "But although it's wonderful to have another little girl, this doesn't mean that we'll forget about Kalle.

"When she died, I was so low that I thought I'd never get back up again. But we're slowly getting there.

"And I know Kalle is still with us. Just the other night, I asked her for a cuddle and felt her arms around me."

In conclusion Karen says of her brush with mediumistic communication: 'Craig and now Spiritualism has given Stan and I the courage to carry on. Our mutual suffering has brought us even closer together. Most of all I like to think that Kalle's over there and, although our time together was short, she may think to herself "I've had two nice parents who adored me".

'Her tragedy has given me an insight into the values of life and if my story of hope in darkness helps just one mother who feels the way I do I will be so happy. There is something far better and far greater that's just that little distance away.

'Kalle has gone home but I know she's always there if I need her.'

Karen is one of the bravest mum's I've met who conquered adversity with dignity and compassion at the loss of her little angel Kalle. For Kalle is indeed an angel for angels are spirits. Constant in every account of angels throughout history is that they are both messengers and companions to humans. Spirits become angels when they are sent. It is the nature of their office to bring messages of the highest hope, inspiration and comfort to those who suffer on earth. Kalle brought this message. She has no wings but she is an angel nonetheless.

Our work as mediums is dedicated to proving that there is life after death. Together, with my wife Jane, who is also a medium, I believe that we have brought comfort and inspiration to many desperate people like Karen who desperately need to know that there is more to this world than just the common place. Jane and I are not New Age gurus and we certainly don't have all the answers to life's many perplexing questions. Sometimes our clairvoyance and mediumship is accurate and precise but there are also times when the clear signals from beyond are clouded by our own thoughts.

I hope that the stories you are about to read may uplift your heart if you are bereaved and inspire those of you who are in search of spiritual truth. In addition I have brought together in this book some of the many incredible stories that I have researched for the British national papers. You will read of the strange stories that have happened to ordinary people who make no claim to having psychic powers. I hope that you will come to realise as you read this book that psychic powers are not just the possession of the few but may indeed be an ancient ability that we have somehow lost as we have become 'civilised'. I hope that this book will open your mind to these powers, encourage you to observe your own sixth sense in action and perhaps even inspire you to unlock and enhance your own latent powers.

I am a reluctant medium. Like many people I had no intention of developing psychic powers, they were thrust upon me. That events of my life sometimes seemed to conspired to push me along this path. It has brought me both joy and woe and, most importantly, shown me that beyond the winding pathways of life lies my spiritual homeland.

DEVELOPING PSYCHIC POWERS

My mother tells me that I've always been psychic. I used to frighten her when I described the things I saw: such as figures in my bedroom at night, colours around people's heads and often had dreams that came true. Also, throughout my life I had an uncanny ability to read peoples thoughts and my telepathic abilities used to astonish, and sometimes frighten, my family and friends.

Of course, mediumistic abilities are more than just mind reading as I will endeavour to prove later. But psychic skills were most certainly with both my wife Jane and I from an early age. In my case they were at first haphazard and it wasn't until I met the medium and police sergeant Peter Close, the brother of England's cricket team captain Brian Close, who trained me in his circle, that the jigsaw puzzle fell into place. It was as if I'd suddenly found what I was searching for all my life and my psychic skills developed at a remarkable rate. Now I knew how to turn the psychic switch on and off and was no longer at the mercy of sometimes unwanted clairvoyant insights.

Soon I could give clear and precise evidence of survival and was able to consciously develop my abilities. Teaching psychic self-development has become an integral part of my work today.

Jane's mediumistic development was quite different. "My grandmother realised that I was a very psychic child" says Jane "she was very interested in psychic things herself, although not a professional medium, she was able to guide my psychic progress. She would do this at first through guessing games and finally taught me to see pictures in a crystal ball which she helped me to interpret. In this way I was able to understand how to develop ESP from an early age"

By the time Jane and I met we were both mediumisticly advanced. It was Jane's dead grandmother who introduced us. I was giving a public demonstration of mediumship in Eastleigh and linked with Jane in the audience. I described and named her grandmother Barber in the spirit who insisted that we meet up. We did; fell in love and were soon married.

Another person who was partly responsible for our coming together was the late medium Doris Stokes:

Thousands thronged to see Doris Stokes's public demonstrations of mediumship. She became the world's best known medium and in her simple, unassuming way popularised the knowledge that had previously been limited only to Spiritualists and other similar organisations. She was famous all over the world and could fill the London Palladium or Sydney Opera House to capacity.

When my sister Vivienne lost her husband from cancer soon after she was married, it was Doris Stokes who helped take the heavy burden of grief from her shoulders. I went with Viv to the sitting and was astonished at the things Doris also said to me.

She 'knew' about my problems as a single parent with a baby of 16 months to look after; she described my grandmother in the spirit world and made some predictions about my business, how I would travel and who and when I would marry.

Two predictions came to pass almost instantly. At the time I was running my own Advertising Agency and she named a blue chip company that I'd be doing work for. A few weeks later, and out of the blue, the company rang me up with a big order that was to put me on a firmer financial footing- Doris had even given me the name of the man who would place the order.

She also said that I'd be going to America with my friend Stuart. Stuart

Martin, a long time friend, was offered a temporary teaching job on an American Youth Camp. As I boarded the plane to LA I recalled what Doris had said.

But the most remarkable prediction that Doris made, although she always said that she couldn't see the future, was concerning my future wife. "Jane Wallis" she had said "You will meet your future wife Jane Wallis on the 6th of March" It took a good few years but it was the 6th of March that Jane and I met at my mediumistic demonstration in Eastleigh. Jane's name was Willis, which was pretty close to Doris's prediction but her grandmother, who pulled the strings from the spirit side, had the maiden name of Wallis. The full story is outlined in my first book *The Psychic Workbook* (Vermilion)

The Stokes family were important to Jane also. "I got to know John Stokes after Doris Stokes had passed to spirit" says Jane "He originally came down to my home in Eastleigh to help a friend of mine who needed some spiritual healing- not many people know about John's healing gift. We got on with each other straight away and often used to meet up, together with his adopted son Terry, at his friend Terry Carter's house in Portsmouth. John was a lovely, kind man and I thought of him as a second father."

Jane's father had died some years ago and when we decided to get married it was John Stokes who Jane asked to give her away in church. We often wonder if Doris Stokes was there too- watching it all from the afterlife.

In fact she was- she told us all about it through another medium:

You can't give yourself a reading- your own thoughts get in the way. So, if Jane and I want to have a message from spirit we have to visit someone else.

There's a psychic shop in Brighton and in part of the shop they have reserved for psychics or mediums to work. Jane was a few months pregnant with Danielle, when we visited, but didn't have as big a bump in front of her. It still wasn't easy to spot she was pregnant.

David Walton was the visiting medium at the shop. We had heard of him but weren't sure if he was genuine or not. It is very hard to find a gifted medium that gets clear evidence and they are not usually inclined to work at the seaside. David Walton proved however to be excellent.

We wanted a sitting together even though we knew that most mediums, including ourselves, prefer to work with sitters independently. There was a cancellation and we were booked in as his last appointment of the day. We were lucky.

"I'm hearing the name Barber" he said going straight to Jane's grandmother's name as I and other mediums had done before. He continued with other good evidence about her and also things from my granddad and various other people we remembered who had gone to spirit. It was all excellent evidence.

"I'm feeling that my guide Dominique wants to come through, "the medium said. Dominique, we were told later, had been a monk in Brussels over 300 years ago and had first appeared to David Walton when he was a boy of 12.

Dominique spoke through David Walton with a gentle, kind voice. He spoke slowly and deliberately with an accent quite different to the mediums.

"Congratulations on the wedding" were his first words. We had not even had our first anniversary. "This baby that's coming is very special. It doesn't belong to you this child it belongs to God. It was no coincidence they way you two came together, you two were chosen for each other. The suffering and pain that both of you have had is for a reason." (Jane had recently nearly died in a major operation)

"You are privileged to have suffered and you have passed the test. On the table laying in front of you are many spiritual gifts and they are yours for the asking. You two are destined and chosen to do this work for God and to lift the burden of suffering from many. Sometimes you may think that we in the spirit have left you but we are always there helping you with your work."

He paused a while and then we heard another voice, a ladies voice with a strong Northern accent.. "Fancy seeing you here love. It's Doris. It was a lovely wedding and John looked so nice beside you. John's not been too well you know and I'm a little worried about what's happening to my Terry." We understood the message as from Doris Stokes for who else would comment on John Stokes or be concerned for their step child Terry.

When David Walton came out of his trance he was surprised that the spirit guides had put him under. He didn't know us from Adam and certainly would never had realised we knew Doris, John, and Terry Stokes. We thanked him for a wonderful sitting and drove home to contemplate what we had been told.

Some time after the sitting Jane, who had gone to bed early, came downstairs where I was watching television. She looked pale faced as she turned off the box and stood in front of the screen to get my attention. "I've just seen the figure of John Stokes stood in our bedroom" she said "He looked happy but I'm sure something has happened to him."

With the hectic schedule we'd been keeping we hadn't contacted John for some time. We'd tried to ring him but the number was dead. The next day I was to do a demonstration of mediumship at The Spiritualist Association of Great Britain at Belgravia Square in London. This had been an old haunt of Doris Stokes so I would ask around when I got there to find out if anyone had any news about John.

"Oh John Stokes," said one of the resident mediums who shared the meditation room, "He passed to spirit only a few week's ago!"

Jane and I believe that sometimes, particularly when we work with an audience, Doris and John work with us from the other side. Perhaps it's just one of those things that many mediums would like to think but I'm sure that they have joined that band of spirit helpers that help both us and other mediums as well. I'm certain that when it's Jane and my turn to go over we'll stand right beside them proving to the people of earth that life really does continue.

DEMONSTRATING MEDIUMSHIP

When the fledgling medium takes their first hesitant flight from the security of the psychic development circle it is nerve-racking. Peter Close, my teacher, kindly introduced me to the Spiritualist Churches he served in London and I was soon to give my first demonstrations to an audience.

Quaking in my boots I stood in front of the congregation at Pembridge Church in London. It was the first time I'd ever been inside a Spiritualist Church let alone take the service! With lots of encouragement from Peter and a sympathetic audience I soon got into my stride and began reeling off details about the spirit communicators. I was amazed how easily and clearly the information came through. With the right 'conditions', as we mediums say, mediumistic communication is much easier.

Modern Spiritualism is generally considered to date from the events which occurred at Hydesville, New York State, U.S.A., on March 31st 1848, when two sisters, Margareta and Catherine Fox established intelligent communication with a spirit entity which had been responsible for noisy rappings in the household. A flood of publicity followed and home circles sprang up in America and, from 1852, in Britain.

The movement began to attract the attention of eminent scientists and intellectuals including Robert Owen (co-founder of the Co-operative movement), Sir William Crookes (a world-famous scientist) and Sir Arthur Conan Doyle (author of the Sherlock Holmes stories). Other intellectual giants joined them and in 1853 the first Spiritualist Church was established at Keighley in Yorkshire, England.

Spiritualism proposed that the spirit world were communicating a new revelation to mankind which had important religious implications. In 1937 the then Archbishop of Canterbury Dr Lang set up a committee to investigate Spiritualism and produced a favourable report. It was suppressed but leaked to Psychic News.

At first it was impossible for mediums to work openly and some mediums such, as Helen Duncan in 1944, were tried and jailed for their beliefs. Spiritualist meetings would be raided by the police and the participants prosecuted under the Vagrancy Act of 1824 and the Witchcraft Act of 1735! It wasn't until as late as 1951 that it became legal to practice mediumship.

I found out all this information long after demonstrating in the Spiritualist Churches. For a long time I had no idea of the extent of Spiritualism or of its intellectual pedigree.

When I took my first Spiritualist service I soon found out what a typical meeting consists of: The medium opens with a prayer and then there's a hymn and a moment of meditation and absent healing. After a short reading the medium then gives a talk about the philosophical implications of spirit communication. This is followed by another hymn to lift the vibrations and finally he gives a demonstration of mediumistic communication for members of the congregation he feels drawn to. As I'd never seen another platform medium in action my style of working was uniquely my own.

Of course I have since taken hundreds of Spiritualist services and today I'm confident when giving a talk or demonstrating mediumship to an audience. To give you an idea of what happens at a demonstration here's a flattering extract from the newsletter of Wilton Spiritualist Church in Wiltshire:

Visiting medium, Craig Hamilton-Parker gave one of the most detailed messages heard in our church at September's meeting. Starting with the name "Hayward" which was initially unrecognised, he then heard the word "Britannia". Keith Williams thought he recognised the details and Craig gave the Christian name of "Colin".

Keith explained that he had served in Ulster with a Colin Hayward, who had been singing "Rule Britannia" just prior to being killed. He had saved his comrades by throwing himself onto an IRA bomb so as to shield the blast. As he did so he sung "Rule Britannia". The message continued:

CHP: "This took place in Londonderry."
KW: "Correct"
CHP: He had a girlfriend and I feel he was just about to get married."
KW: "He was due to go on leave in nine day's time and would have got married three days after that"
CHP: "Do you know if the girl's name was Sally?"
KW: "I can't remember" (This was confirmed as correct later)
CHP: "He's talking about Charlie Watts".
KW: "That was his best friend."
CHP: "There was also a Tommy in the group he saved. Quite gangling in his appearance."
KW: "That's right."
CHP: "He's showing me his cap-badge. It has three feathers on it."
KW: "Yes he was in the Hussars."
CHP: "I'm getting the 23rd September"
KW: "As far as I can remember, he died in late September."

Now that's the sort of evidence Spiritualism really stands on. In my 30 years in the movement, I have rarely heard such detailed 'evidence of identity'.

Well, there's a feather in my cap too.

Spiritualists are lovely people but I feel sad for the movement as a whole. Unfortunately Spiritualism's glorious past has in some ways stopped it progressing. Today most of the intellectuals have deserted it, materialisation circles are now extremely rare and even the standards of mental mediumship have deteriorated to superficial psychism. But perhaps the death knell for Spiritualism is that it is so old fashioned and is plagued by committees that cannot agree on the simplest agenda for change. The net effect is that Spiritualism can sometimes be boring.

Despite this however, there are still pockets of excellence within the movement that may in the future bring about a re animation and new momentum. Spiritualism at its best can be tremendously uplifting and at its worse is dull and shallow. Despite its faults though it's well worth looking into- maybe you can help change it?

I have a great deal to thank Spiritualism for. Peter Close is himself a Spiritualist and the Spiritualist Church gave me a platform to practice my skills in front of the public. Without this experience it would have been far more difficult to work as confidently as I do today on television, the radio and through the newspapers.

Jane's early development was quite different: Guided by her Grandmother during childhood the bond continued after Grandmother died. "I've always felt that my grandmother draws close at important times" says Jane "Sometimes she advises or warns me about events and there have been occasions when I've heard her voice give such a clear warning that I act upon it. Craig and I have even turned down television shows if my grandmother's spirit has said it's a negative show. She was certainly right when we turned down what looked like a golden opportunity to become well known. The show in question we saw later was hosted by the American conjuror James Randi. He is an arch sceptic and gave everyone a hard time."

As I was developing a reputation as a medium who demonstrates to an audience Jane's reputation was spreading because of her private sittings. Before we became professional, we never charged for our public or private work.

Jane, I know, has saved many despairing people from the brink of suicide. Sometimes the overwhelming influence of the spirit people and the insistence of her 'dead' grandmother would impel her to rush to people's houses unannounced. Sometimes she would turn up just in the nick of time:

The telephone directory lay open on the living room table when Jane saw the vivid blue light flash across it. She picked it up and the blue lights highlighted the name of J Chivers.

"I knew that something was desperately wrong at this unknown persons house" says Jane recalling the events of 1972 "I felt the spirit of a young boy close to me and heard my Grandmother urging that I should go straight away to the address. His father was in desperate need of assistance."

Jane jumped in the taxi and instead of going to the supermarket as she had planned that afternoon, drove directly to Mr Chivers address. "It was a hard house to find, but on route I could hear the spirit voice giving me precise directions. Turn left here, right there, straight on at the lights etc." continues Jane.

Jim Chivers, from Bitterne, Southampton, remembers the day well. "Jane knocked our door and said 'Is your name Jim? Have you lost a little boy of fifteen called Tim?'."

Jim's young son, Tim, had quite recently been killed in a road accident on his way home from school. He'd fallen off his bike as he rode up a hill and was crushed under the wheels of a lorry. The ambulance rushed him to hospital but within four hours he was dead.

"Jane unexpectedly gave me a wealth of evidence that proved that Tim was now safe in the spirit world." says Jim "My wife Shirley and I could never have made it without the assistance of people like Jane. Over the years from the evidence of mediums and spiritualists I have grown to understand that death is by no means the end. Life does indeed continue and, although I am still depressed sometimes on Tim's birthday, passing and at Christmas, I know that he is safely in God's hands."

"I think that anybody that's not had a bereavement can explain the loss you feel." says Jim "Although its a disgusting and selfish thing to do, I made two attempts a suicide but realise now that the grief I and my family endured was for a purpose- so that I could understand what others go through and offer help."

"The hardest part was driving home from hospital without a son" continues Jim, "You know it's happened but can't believe it.

In my despair I turned to my local Christian Church but found no solace there. I realised that the vicar's knew nothing about the afterlife even though they talk about it in their sermons every Sunday."

Jim Chivers sought out other mediums to help him with his grief. "I saw mediums Phil Thomas, Mary Clifford and other spiritualists. Their reassurance and evidence- Tim kept coming through- built my strength further."

"Now I don't need the evidence. I'm thankful for the guidance that the spirit world have given me through mediums like Jane."

Tim's loss has since opened a wonderful spiritual door for Jim. Once he became stronger he joined a psychic development group and discovered that he too has the gifts of clairvoyance, mediumship and healing. Jim has become a close friend of Jane and I and, since his retirement, has become a superb medium who understands the terrible suffering that many of his own sitters are experiencing.

"My own grief has meaning if it has taught me to lift the burden from another's shoulders" he concludes.

I know how much Jane's mediumship and the work of the Spiritualists helped Jim come to terms with the loss of his son. Jim is a very sincere man and a follower of the Indian Avatar Sathya Sai Baba who you will read about in the last chapter of this book. During his time of grief he was very vulnerable and a false psychic could have wrought terrible damage.

Fortunately in Jane he met the right person. But there are also many sham psychics around:

Soon after her aunt Olive died Sue Pedrick (35) from Southampton decided to visit a medium to see if Olive could communicate with her. "I needed to know if I was making the best plans for her mentally handicapped son Graham" says Sue "If only Olive could let me know that she approved of my plans and agreed that what I was doing was in Graham's best interest."

Sue's husband Cliff (43) accompanied her to the consultation in Fareham but wasn't impressed. "Frankly it was an absolute load of twaddle." says Cliff "The woman said things that could apply to anyone and made a string of predictions- none of which have happened. We came away feeling cheated"

Three months later Sue decided that she'd like to try again to contact Olive but this time Cliff insisted that they apply some rules. "We'd read about the Eastleigh based medium Craig Hamilton-Parker and made an appointment to see him" says Cliff "But this time we weren't going to be taken in. Sue and I agreed that we wouldn't lead the medium or give anything away. We agreed that we would only answer 'yes', 'no' or 'don't know'."

But Cliff and Sue were pleased at what I told them "No sooner had I sat down, than Craig told me that he was in touch with my father. He said he saw him with jet black hair like mine but had brilliant blue eyes He eventually died of a chest infection said Craig but spoke in whispers because there had been something seriously wrong with his throat."

Just before Cliff's father died he had contracted cancer of the throat and had his voice box removed. "Everything Craig said was true yet I had deliberately given him no clues." continues Cliff, "I could hardly believe what I was hearing."

Next I turned to Sue and said that he wanted to give her a message from her mother. "Craig told me how she died and gave the date of her death to within a few days. He told me that her pet poodle dog was with her and she was now showing him a picture of Michael Jackson. Mum loved her poodle and only two days before my five year old son Vincent had impersonated Michael Jackson for the school play.

"'She's joking about your middle name' I said 'Can you understand Yan?' My middle name is Yana which dad had chosen because he loved the music of the singer of the same name. Everyone, including mum, used to pull my leg about it.

"Craig went on to say that mum was telling him to say that I mustn't worry too much about the twin's asthma and that my bad back would improve. I then stopped and said that he was going to ask mum for some information that would give me absolute proof that he was in touch with her. 'She's showing me lots of little silver horseshoes'

"Before mum died she had worked with me in my catering business. After every wedding she would ask the bride for permission to take a silver horseshoe off the cake for good luck. Mum soon had a huge collection of silver horse shoes."

But the spirit world hadn't finished. There were others who also wanted to communicate. "Craig asked me if I knew of a Steve in the spirit world. Of course I did it was my brother! Steve, as Craig was saying, had taken his own life. He had taken an overdose and the drugs said Craig were medically prescribed but they belonged to someone else.

"This was quite correct. Craig went on to describe his character, how he liked motorbikes and how we played his favourite song by Meatloaf at his funeral. The fake medium we'd seen in Fareham was using guesswork but these were hard facts that nobody could deny."

Eventually, when the consultation was almost coming to a close, aunt Olive made contact. "Craig wasn't able to give Olive's name but he was able to correctly say that she was a somewhat domineering school teacher. We'd played the music from her school assembly at the funeral. 'The music was something about a train' Craig said The first line of the song was 'Train whistle blowing'!

"He also accurately described her cancer and how her leg swelled." continues Sue "But the information that really shocked me most was when Craig said that she was dressed in pink in the coffin. Then Craig turned to Cliff and said 'And all thanks to you Cliff, you were the one who dressed her'"

"Most people leave jobs like that to the undertakers" says Cliff "But Olive always looked like a million dollars in life and I intended that she see out her last moments in style. I dressed her in her finest jewellery and favourite pink dress and jacket.

"Then Craig turned to Sue and said 'And talking about clothes, you've gone from rags to riches. You're now a regular Imelda Marcos.' Craig was spot on again A few months before she died Olive had sold her house and went on a massive shopping spree. Sue inherited her clothes which included 8 unopened boxes of new shoes and about another 40 pairs of used ones."

"Craig said that I'd had her wedding ring made smaller so that her son Graham could wear it and that she now had something very important to say 'She's saying' said Craig 'that you've done nothing wrong for Graham, in fact she's very pleased with what you've done and organised."

This was the vital piece of information that Sue and Cliff had been longing to hear. Although Graham lives in care, Sue and Cliff have made him part of their own family. He comes to stay regularly and particularly loves staying for the New Year. "We're both convinced now that life goes on after death" concludes Sue "But it's equally comforting to know that the people we love who've passed over can see and comment on the work that we continue in their memory."

As Cliff and Sue's story illustrates, you have to be so wary of which clairvoyant you choose to see. A bad one or an outright charlatan can put you off for life. I've been told some terrible things by the fakes. As an adolescent a 'psychic' said that I'd break my back before I was twenty and another said that I'd die of lung cancer and another said that I'd loose a leg and another said that I'd have my stomach removed. (Thank God they left me with the important bits.) In every case they weren't able to give me any evidence to prove what they were saying had substance. They didn't tell me anything about my past or present yet could make these terrible outlandish predictions about my future.

Jane had a similar experience when she saw a 'clairvoyant' at the seaside on the Isle of Wight. "Your having an affair" the seer said with utmost confidence. Jane became quite angry with her as she fervently believes that infidelity is wrong. (Jane and I may verbally demolish each other if we have a row and we certainly don't have a marriage made in heaven but we both know that we'd never let each other down through adultery. We both had enough of that from our first marriage partners.) When Jane told her she was wrong the clairvoyants reply was "Well that surprises me, nearly everyone that comes to see me does"

Clearly the woman concerned was using guesswork. And bad psychics say that they never get it wrong or attempt to make things fit with the flimsiest of evidence. We all get it wrong sometimes or get our lines crossed. Jane and I can immediately spot a bad clairvoyant but people like this can be really upsetting for someone who assumes that person giving the reading has an infallible gift:

"My life was a mess and everything was going wrong. I was deeply depressed and didn't know where to turn. In desperation I decided to visit a psychic." says Susie Fabian from Alton in Hampshire." But what the psychic told me was so terribly upsetting- in fact quite terrifying- that I cried all the way home."

Susie knows now that the woman she saw was a complete charlatan. "She would listen carefully to what I gave away and feed it back to me later in the consultation. For example I mentioned that I lived in the countryside. Ten minutes later she told me that there were horses near where I lived and I should drive a Land Rover. She fished for information and then started predicting the most frightening things that were to happen: I'd lose my job, husband, home, money, health- you name it- I'd be losing it. 'I'd like to tell you something positive my dear but I can't' said the seer."

For ages Susie kept what she was told to herself. "I worried about what I was told day and night" she says "It wasn't until I shared my feelings with my close friend Liz that I began to see how I'd been conned. I played her the tape and we soon realised when we analysed it that she was telling me things I'd already mentioned earlier."

Angrily Susie's friend destroyed the tape in front of her

"But despite this bad encounter I still wanted to see a psychic and Liz recommended Craig. He had seen many of her friends.

"Craig explained that he wanted firstly to communicate with the spirit world and ask them about my life. He started telling me about my mother who had died a few years ago. He said how she hadn't changed much and even though money was not important where she was she still worried about it as she was penniless when she died. He told me when she died, how she died, named names and what she was like as a person. Mum laughed about Dad- how he lived on sandwiches, refused to budge from the house and told me lots of stories of things that happened in my life. These were absolutely accurate and no one in a million years could guess the facts but also they are very personal to me and I would rather keep them to myself. Suffice it is to say- I knew by now that some, but not all, psychics are true."

After the mediumistic work I offered to use the Tarot cards to look into Susie's future. I am first and foremost a medium but sometimes people need a little extra guidance. I believe that the future is subject to our own free will- we can change it. Many mediums disagree with fortune telling because of the harrowing stories you hear of deception. In the right hands Tarot Cards can be a useful tool- but that's all they are, a tool to help with precognition. I see them as a way to compose a philosophy that the sitter can apply to their circumstances. Ultimately the future's what you make it.

The oracle showed problems ahead for Susie but they weren't impossible. With the guidance of spirit Susie made a plan of action to make the best of the circumstances available. I believe that if you sincerely put love behind your actions, then inevitably you will do the right thing and in time reap the benefit.- it's the natural law of things.

"I left Craig's house on a high" says Susie "Inside I felt at peace with myself. I knew that there were problems to deal with in my life. It wasn't going to be a bed of roses but now I could cope."

SPIRITUAL BIRTH

When Jane and I met and married our lives started to change. Jane fell pregnant with our daughter but four months into her pregnancy on Christmas Eve she collapsed at home. I was urgently called to the hospital. 'We have X rayed your wife' said the consultant 'and have discovered a large growth.' When I pressed to know if it was cancer the consultant would not answer one way or the other. They would operate tomorrow- Christmas

Day. It was likely, they warned, that she would lose the baby.

Perhaps the worst moment for both of us was having to leave Jane alone in hospital. Our children from our previous marriage were looking forward to Father Christmas coming. It was too late to make arrangements with their Grandparents so I returned home to get them to bed, wrap the presents and fill the stockings. Jane was very brave and faced the forthcoming crisis with great courage. Our first Christmas together as a family was not to be.

On Christmas morning the surgeons removed an ovarian cyst from Jane's fallopian tubes. It was one of the biggest they'd ever seen. And it was benign!

"I was worried that there might be complications with my pregnancy" says Jane "I was 38 and some people think that that's too old to have a baby But both Craig and I had been married before and we wanted a child of our own. We decided that the birth should reflect our spiritual values"

When Jane announced that she wanted to have the baby at home by underwater birth I thought that she was joking. In theory it sounded a great idea but after the hospital scare I would have preferred that she had as 'normal' a birth as possible with as much technology around us as a hospital could muster.

But Jane would have none of it. Her mind was made up.

The midwife reassured me that if there were any complications then they would take Jane straight to hospital. Gradually I relented. There were many benefits: it reduces pain of the mother's contractions and eases the trauma of birth for the baby. And many claim that a water birth improves a child's intelligence and makes them more perceptive - even psychic. But most of all it symbolised a spiritual entry into the world. Water is a very powerful conductor of psychic energies and if Jane and I were in the pool together then our auras, and spirits would blend together.

"The birthing pool was a round blue plastic tub of about 6 ft in diameter that came in four sections- it looked like a deep paddling pool." says Jane "Craig, who normally detests DIY, assembled it and we filled it up for a practice run. Celeste (Craig's daughter from his first marriage) and Chantal (my first daughter) were dying to get in to our new swimming pool that had taken over our dining room. Even our dog William barked his frustration at not being able to join in the fun. For the practice run we could be carefree but for the birth itself we were careful to sterilise everything. We were supplied with a special sterile lining to be used on the big day. The midwife was very cautious to ensure that the extensive training she had undertaken at her own expense, to plan for this birth, was put fully into effect.

"For the trial run I put an ugly 'cabbage patch doll' under my T-shirt and when I pushed it out, with realistic groans of birth, it would shoot to the surface like a cork. 'Oh look mummy it looks just like Craig' said Chantal sarcastically. I couldn't wait for the real baby to come along ,everybody was excited even the midwife.

"On the morning of the 22nd June, the day after the Summer Solstice, I started to get contractions. Then they stopped. I started to experience terrible pain and Craig quickly rang the midwife and began filling the pool. When Jan arrived the baby was well on its way and it was touch and go as to whether we could fill the pool at the right temperature of exactly 100 degrees Fahrenheit in time. Our central heating system and immersion heater were having trouble coping. And so was I

"The midwife could feel with her hand that the baby was facing the wrong way and that if it didn't turn, they might have to use forceps. The pain was, for a time, unbearable but as soon as I got into the water the pain in my back just went and the baby's head engaged round the correct way. I wished that I'd got in earlier. Craig shut the blinds, put on some tranquil new age music, put on his bathers and leaped in with me. He held me from behind to give me an anchor to push against. The midwife rang everyone that should be there. And Doctor Hood, our GP, brought along his little boy to watch.

"Then the doorbell rang. It was our daughters Chantal and Celeste back from school. They too came into the room to watch the birth and could help if they wanted. Chantal decided not to have a ring side view watch but watched through the part opened dinning room door. Celeste absolutely loved it. She sponged my forehead and insisted on watching everything. There would never be any rivalry or jealousy towards this baby, I thought, they had helped deliver it!"

I never realised that when a woman is giving birth she has the strength of ten men. I too felt like ten men but nine of them were dead. Every time Jane pushed against the side with her legs she pushed against my chest. (she was sitting in my lap) With each contraction all the air would be forced out of my lungs and together with the weight of the water I felt that I was going to start hyperventilating or something. I laughed to myself and thought "So you wanted to share the experience of the birth now you've got it pain and all". It was also amusing the way Celeste kept coming over and mopping my brow while Jane sweated away unattended. Afterwards Jane looked fine and as if nothing had happened, everyone said that I looked like the one who had given birth!

At 4.26 PM the baby arrived. "I put my hands down into the water and delivered her myself." says Jane proudly "I took hold of the head when I felt it drop. The midwife was pleased to see that the baby was now in the correct position and had fully turned while I was in the water. I gently lifted the baby up through the surface of the water. It was a beautiful moment, as if time stood still. A holy moment. I was ecstatic as I pulled the baby upwards as if in slow motion- it was a girl. The moment she was out of the water she began to cry and I started laughing-she was perfect in every detail. We'd suffered so much and now here was our little baby."

The girls were amazed. We thought that they might have been squeamish but they really loved watching the birth. "Well done" said my mum, arriving only seconds after the birth. She was the first to hold the baby. "This is how a birth should be" says Jane "with your family gathered round you. I climbed out of the tub to deliver the afterbirth in private. (much to the disappointment of Celeste who wanted to see more) I had a few stitches but it was remarkable that I had needed no gas or painkillers throughout. The girls eagerly nursed baby Danielle, and we all had a nice cup of tea. We needed it as it was a very hot day, the tubs water was 100 degrees, it was about 80 outside, and the whole building was as hot and steamy as a sauna.

"There was a wonderful atmosphere in that house that day." says Jane "It was very special. The doctor and midwife looked all flaked out. Already I was thinking how I'd like to do it all over again. A water birth at home is a truly spiritual experience. I didn't feel tired but they made me have a bath and go to bed.

"I lay in bed I looked at baby Danielle snuggled in my arms. Here was this beautiful darling little baby with lots of hair and so perfect in every way. I truly believed that she was a child of God. My Danielle. My water baby. I was so pleased that at last our child had arrived. When I looked into her brilliant blue eyes' says Jane 'I knew that all the suffering was worthwhile.'

But the suffering was by no means over. A few days after Danielle was born we received papers from the courts telling us that both of our ex-partners were filing for custody of the step children. Jane's ex-husband was engaged to an American multi millionairess so money was no object. Meanwhile my ex-wife was on legal aid. We fought tooth and nail but the financial consequences of the long drawn out court cases were crippling.

I can't go into details but it hurt us all to see the new family broken up. I had struggled for 9 years on my own bringing Celeste up from 16 months old and making tremendous sacrifices to ensure she was all right. Jane had also made similar sacrifices over Justin and Chantal

My advertising agency, which I had toiled to establish over 15 years, began to suffer because of the time I had to spend in court and in preparing to go to court. I missed critical meetings and couldn't follow up sales leads. Instead of writing quotes I wrote affidavits. Turn-over plummeted and costs rose. Then I lost my three most important accounts within a week. The business collapsed.

As I watched the receiver tow away my Jaguar car I clearly heard the voice of my 'dead' Grandmother. 'Don't worry Craig. It's only things. Go forward now and do what you know you've got to do.'

Somehow we kept our house and survived. In the space of a year our world had changed beyond recognition. No more champagne lunches entertaining clients at French restaurants; no more trips for Jane on the QE2, no more luxuries. But deep in our hearts we knew that these things didn't matter. Spiritually we had both already decided to dedicate our lives to the service of Spirit. Now was our chance to prove it in cold reality.

The decks had been cleared and the stage was set for a new beginning. In a few years we'd been through some momentous times. Nothing much more could be taken away from us. The only way was up.

NEXT WEEK'S NEWS TODAY

A career as full time medium is not easy. If you're sincere in your work it's not possible to work every day- you need time to recharge or you burn yourself out. And even if your schedule is full, people fail to turn up or you feel that you can't charge them because they too are in difficulties. So it was important to have another string to our bow. I had advertising skills, copywriting skills and understood Public Relations. My thoughts turned to writing and television.

Our big break came when Bob Geldoff's TV production company Planet

24 rang us to audition for a new programme to be screened early mornings on Channel 4 and to be called *The Big Breakfast*. We were to be their resident psychics. Each week we would appear with Paula Yates and predict the coming week's news headlines.

At the 'job interview' Jane and I gave private sittings to two of the most sceptical producers so that they could ascertain whether we were psychic or not before we did a screen test. Both of them were shaken by how much we could tell them about their lives and people they knew in the spirit, indeed the young man I gave a reading to was so emotionally overwhelmed that he requested if he could take a little time off to come to terms with what he'd just experienced.

Next we did a screen test to camera in which we would make our predictions for the coming week. The camera crew laughed when Jane said that one of the Queen's beloved corgis would die but this prophesy and most of the other predictions we made all came to pass within the week.

We got the job.

I'm sure Paula Yates was just itching to tear us apart from the moment she first saw us come onto the brightly coloured set to the tones of the music from *The Twilight Zone*. It's her Taurean instinct. But time after time our predictions were spot on and soon even she accepted that what we were doing couldn't be dismissed as cleaver guesswork. We foresaw world events with an accuracy that amazed everyone including sometimes ourselves. We predicted the El Al air tragedy in Holland, the birth of 'miracle' Siamese twins who were separated, that Princess Anne would marry and the venue would be Scotland, the Queen being hit by an egg, haemophiliac blood contaminated in France; men walking to the South Pole; Elizabeth Taylor's heart attack; Rembrandt drawings found; a mock assassination attempt on Ross Perot; the French farmers' lamb protest; Cliff Richard losing his voice; a boy impaled on railings; Mafia boss Totto seized; footballer Paul Gascoigne getting a black eye; cult leader Koresh killing himself; Chris Patten having an heart attack; the horse ripper attacks; oil tankers colliding off Indonesia; and an unscheduled meeting of the Queen with Boris Yeltsin.

Chris Evans, Paula Yates, Gabby Rossiter, the crew and even the owner Waheed Ali all became very interest in what we were doing and occasionally asked for predictions about their own lives. Chris told us that he was quite open to psychic things ever since his mother became very interested in spiritual healing.

PSYCHIC ENCOUNTERS

At the first *Big Breakfast* party we were so swamped by people wanting impromptu readings that we nearly missed all the fun. Waheed Ali and Charlie Parsons had, it was rumoured, spent over £20,000 to make sure we were all rewarded for making the show such a huge success.

It was an amazing party. They hired a disused factory that had three floors. The first floor was decked out as heaven with stained glass windows angels and the like, the ground was purgatory with a 20 ft pair of hands pointing to heaven and to the Hell in the basement. In 'Hell' you could get drinks and candy floss if you bought 'Bank of Spank' currency from any of the chain smoking nuns wearing sunglasses. Various performers entertained throughout the building including a bizarre surrealistic pageant of ballroom dancers smiling gaily at the crowds.

This, in my opinion was their best party although a close second must be the boxing party which synchronised our celebrations with Frank Bruno's world championship challenge against Mike Tyson in America. In the centre of the party was a boxing ring in which the entertainment took place and we all stopped to watch Bruno fight on a massive screen that showed the fight live from America. Everyone placed a bet for a big prize and of course many people asked what Jane and I predicted. We didn't have the heart to bet on anyone except the magnanimous Frank Bruno who we'd got to know briefly on the show. He lost.

The *Big Breakfast* was great fun and certainly got us known quickly. It was also exciting mixing with the famous and every week we seemed to meet another mega-star. It was so casual. I spent quite a while talking to someone who I thought was part of the crew. "I recognise that bloke" I said to Jane innocently as we climbed the stairs to the dressing room.

"That 'bloke' is Patrick Swayze stupid. You know, the one that stared in your favourite film *Ghost*!" But Jane is used to this she knows my legendary bad memory for names and faces.

A similar situation happened when the pop group *Take That* appeared on the show. They'd just hit the charts with their first single and we'd never heard of them. I think they must have found it amusing when Jane, thinking that they were young 'runners', sent Robbie off to fetch her a cup of coffee. Surprisingly he obeyed without a murmur!

It's times like this that you realise that you're getting older.

But the star that impressed us most must be the boxer Frank Bruno. When he cottoned on that we were the show's psychics he started pulling Jane's leg about being the 'Vibe Lady'. Frank was pure gold and had us all laughing at his witty quips that were as quick as his punches.

We also met the boxer Chris Eubanks on the show but he was a little more serious to say the least. He nearly bit Jane's head off when she said "You know money's not everything Chris". Clearly money is pretty important to him. However, we had a very interesting conversation with him about 'the warrior spirit' just before, in serious mood, he strutted off for his interview with Paula Yates.

Paula wiped the floor with him.

Most of the stars we met were as you would expect them to be. Oliver Reed was looking for the drinks cabinet, Glenda Jackson never lifted her head from the newspaper and Jason Donovan was as immaculate as his posters. Kylie Minogue was a bit of a shock though because you just don't expect a mega star to be quite that small! And super model Naiomi Cambell looked great until she opened her mouth. To camera she speaks in a convincing transatlantic accent. Off stage, her accent is from deepest Streatham.

Tom Jones and his manager son were surprisingly approachable and we enjoyed our dressing room chats with Billy Joe Spears, Rupert Everett and Brother Beyond. Only a few months ago we'd never been into a TV studio except to take part in *Kilroy*. Now we were mixing with the stars every week. When Doris Stokes had told me at my private consultation with her that I'd marry a girl called Jane and that together we'd be two of the world's top mediums I never really believed it. But here it was. It had all started to come true.

The *Big Breakfast* was tremendous experience for us. It was a groundbreaking style of production that required supreme confidence of delivery. The time allocated to do our bit was worked out to the second so we had to get it right first time and, at the same time, let our personalities shine through. We jumped in at the deep end and swam. After the frantic live TV style of the *Big Breakfast* any other TV we would do would be easy.

Soon our faces were familiar to viewers and there followed a flood of television offers interested in our psychic and mediumistic work. Working for regional, network and cable companies, we soon found ourselves being driven or flown all over the country to take part in various features with a paranormal theme. Some of our predictions on Channel 4 were even screened on Fox Television in America.

We did the chat shows. Comfy pink settees at the crack of dawn. And inevitably we would be asked to demonstrate our psychic skills to titillate the viewers. For *This Morning* with Richard Madaley we demonstrated flower reading and psychometry successfully and then gave psychic readings to people who rang the show. We were told not to do mediumship as 'it may be a little too serious for a light entertainment show' but considering the pressure to 'perform' our accuracy on the phone was very good.

Richard Madeley felt quite armoured toward psychic phenomena. He admitted that like most people with a journalistic or media training he was taught to be sceptical but believed we 'have tremendous guts standing up in front of a camera and doing what you do. I find it all hard to believe.' On the same show to promote a new book was the famous journalist and one time editor of the *Daily Express* Eve Pollard who was, to my surprise, very sociable, humorous and apparently open minded about the existence of extra sensory perception.

Fortunately before we'd gone on *This Morning* we'd already had loads of practice at phone-ins. For nearly a year we had practised giving telephone readings over the air for our local commercial radio station South Coast Radio. In this case it was a late night show and nobody worried if we talked about the spirit world or demonstrated mediumship. If only mainstream television were so open minded! For *The Cheryl Buggy Show* we were able to give some really uplifting evidence of survival. It was the sort of heart felt material that could bring a lump to your throat. Sometimes we could give the full names of the spirit communicator, how they died and an accurate description of their personality. In addition we were able to give exact evidence of stories from their lives. For example I remember one caller, with a Wiltshire accent challenge us to say which musical instrument her father had played before he died. "The bagpipes!!" chirped up Jane. I remember we were also able to tell one caller that he had a leg missing, another that she was looking at a picture of her mother as she spoke yet all we had as a 'link' was an unfamiliar voice at the end of the phone line and the guidance of spirit.

Every time we appeared on the show the switchboard was jammed with calls.

We demonstrated psychometry and did a phone in for Meridian TV's *Late Night Live* with presenters Penny Smith from GMTV and John Leslie from *Blue Peter*. For this somewhat hectic show we read the vibrations from various objects including a glass eye! On set we also met our old friend Graham Rogers who's we had got to know when we gave guest appearances on his all night link programme *Nightime*.

We did a series of shows for *UK Living* with Jane Irving, demonstrated aura reading, phone ins and interpreted dreams. For *The Vanessa Show* we gave readings to people in the audience and interpreted what they were feeling by the colours of their aura. Afterwards there was a heated debate with one man getting quite irate about how people like us are frauds. We all really let of steam and it was an exciting show.

We went on the *Richard and Judy* chat show and for the Daily Mirror's cable programme *L!VE TV* I taught astral projection and Jane demonstrated how to use the crystal ball. Normally in television what you say is edited down to just a few minutes but on cable there's so much time to fill that you pretty well have as much time as you like. I even went on *Newsnight* to make predictions about the General Election.

One show that was a complete disaster was Sky's *One to Three*. I'd written a feature called 'The Twilight Bone' for *The Sunday Mirror* in which I related various stories that proposed that pets have a sixth sense. The programme producers suggested that we set up a TV experiment in which Jane and I would use telepathy to will a **hungry** dog to eat from the bowl of our choice. Unfortunately the woman who supplied the dog fed him just before he came on and, to our horror, continued feeding him titbits right up to the moment we released him for the experiment.

The dog took no interest in the food whatsoever.

It soon became clear to us that British television is divided into two distinctive camps: 'entertainment and 'documentary'. Unless it's being trashed by magicians, psychologists and journalists, television rarely makes serious programmes about the type of work we do. Even the investigative programmes are still considered as entertainment. It's terribly frustrating when you consider the spiritual implications of what we are trying to say.

And as the Spiritualists have discovered to their cost, the media just aren't interested in the philosophical gauntlet that proof of life after death throws into the arena. It is almost impossible to put forward a case for mediumship. For a long time the BBC refused to screen anything remotely connected with clairvoyance or mediumship. Even today, a contrary viewpoint from the sceptics always has to be put forward at the same time. I wonder how the public would react if it was mandatory that every time a clergyman expressed an opinion on air then an atheist, psychologist or magician must give an alternative viewpoint. I can see it in the listings: 'Songs of Praise: tonight's programme includes a talk by the archbishop and a demonstration of water walking by James Randi.'

As we have never had a theatrical agent it is perhaps inevitable that we were never paid particularly well for our TV work. The entertainment programmes were fun and useful but really we wanted to reach out to people and let them know about the serious and compassionate side of our work.

The opportunity came firstly through the newspapers when I signed a contract with *The Scottish Daily Record* to write a column idea I had proposed to them. I suggested that I write it in Jane and my name and call it *The Psychic Postbag* It would answer readers questions about psychic subjects and quote their experiences. The resulting weekly Saturday page was flooded with letters telling sometimes amazing stories. The Scots, perhaps because of their Celtic roots and the tradition of highland seership, were very open to what we had to say and the *Psychic Postbag* became a lively, informative and sometimes touching column. Throughout Scotland it caused quite a stir.

When Grampian Television's producers in Aberdeen, who had read the column, suggested that I host a serious debate called *We the Jury* I was delighted to at last be able to put forward some serious ideas. The theme we chose was 'Is there life after death?'. I would put forward my argument then a well known journalist put a contrary viewpoint.

For my witnesses I called doctors (who spoke about out of body experiences), Spiritualists, Swedenbourg followers, the Society of Psychical Research and representatives of different faiths. I had planned the debate well and the usual sceptics, psychologists and magicians in the opposing camp were soon demolished. The telephone poll, that was to decide who had won the argument, was overwhelmingly in my favour. In fact, the presenter said that it was the biggest majority the programme had ever seen.

Perhaps programme makers should note that the public are really very interested in the philosophical implications of clairvoyance and mediumship.

Soon afterwards we were both whisked off to Scotland to be the main guests on Scottish Television's popular programme titled *Scottish Women*. I demonstrated mediumship to the audience and gave some convincing proof. Jane gave private consultations to some members of the audience selected by the producers. Again without telling us, the same person was also given a 'tarot' reading by a psychologist posing as a clairvoyant.

Afterwards the people who had been given the readings were asked for their opinions. They had no idea that the other reader was a psychologist. Everyone agreed that Jane's reading was spot on but that the psychologist had said things that were so general that it could apply to anyone. When my mediumistic demonstration was picked apart it was found that everything I had said was perfectly correct.

Once again Jane and I had confounded the sceptics.

I can understand why so many psychics and mediums find that their powers aren't there when they try and demonstrate on TV. Producers are sneaky. They tell you that they are making a sympathetic programme then confront you with psychologists, sceptics and debunkers. You never know what to expect and consequently most psychics are understandably unnerved when this type of thing happens to them on a show. Fortunately, Jane and I have now done so much television that it now takes quite a lot to make us fail. Most of the time we know what to expect.

Another debate that I enjoyed was filmed in Birmingham for *Central Tonight*. They packed me off to a location that a local psychic had said that a murder had taken place. I was supposed to find the body. I felt nothing and as far as I was concerned the local medium had got it wrong. I met the mother of the murdered girl and I remember telling her that a place by the name of Cromwell was important. The name meant nothing but a few years later dead bodies were discovered at Cromwell Road in nearby Gloucester. They were the victims of the serial killers Fred and Rosemary West. However I've had no direct confirmation that the young girl was one of their serial victims.

Central Tonight was a lively debate which I co-hosted with the excellent medium Stephen O'Brian and argued our case against the unlikely bedfellows of Susan Blackmore, a psychologist from Bristol University and a vicar. Susan Blackwell put forward her usual arguments about hallucinations caused by the temporal lobes and the vicar told everyone what an evil lot we are.

This was not the first occasion we've had been asked to use our psychic powers in conjunction with a murder. Winnie Johnson who lost her son to the serial killers Ian Bradey and Maura Hindley contacted us through the *Big*

Breakfast to see if we could help her find her son Keith's body that had been hidden on the moors since the 1960's. Winnie spoke to Jane who was able to tell her a few things about her son over the phone that had never been revealed such as the fact that he was on his way to the opticians on the day he was abducted.

Jane was able to relay a few of her feelings about the whereabouts of the body but Saddleworth Moors is a huge, bleak place and Keith's body is still unfound. It's a heartbreaking fact that poor Winnie Johnson has scoured the moors every weekend since she lost her son in 1964. She said to Jane "If I could just hug my little boy's bones I would be at peace"

Keith's mum told how she is still haunted by the screams of little Leslie Ann begging for life and crying for her mother that she heard from recordings made by Brady and Hindley. They tortured and sexually abused the tied up children. In the background of the tape could be heard Christmas carols and the barking commands of Brady for the child to pose in sexually explicit positions. For Winnie Johnson the nightmare will never end. Some say that Maura Hindley should now be released from prison. I think not.

One of Jane and my best shows together was *Something Strange* for HTV in Bristol. For this one we were billed as mediums and were given the opportunity to demonstrate what we're best at- mediumship. We both gave very accurate proof of who we were communicating with and gave the correct names of the spirit person being described. For example I said to one lady in the audience "Your mother's in the spirit. Her name's Alice and she tells me that you've just bought a small yacht and are going to soon open a delicatessen shop" which was correct. And Jane told someone that she knew of "A fireman who had just hurt his back in a skiing accident" which was also correct.

Again there was the obligatory sceptic. This time they employed a magician who demonstrated sleight of hand to 'prove' that mediums, an particularly materialisation mediums, can employ trickery. Frankly, to put forward an argument based upon a few camera tricks was ridiculous and the audience knew it.

The medium Doris Collins also took part and was filmed giving some one-to-one readings in a private room. I've seen her do better and afterwards she seemed to be very snappy towards us. However, despite this, I believe that all the clairvoyants and mediums who took part, collectively gave some pretty convincing proof that it really is possible to prove that there is life after death.

Working under the hot lights of the studio and being told where to walk and stand and exactly when and how long to speak is of course not the perfect way to demonstrate mediumship. Television producers have no idea how ambient and subtle the spirit voices can be. They wrongly assume that we can switch our powers off and on to order. So when the makers of a programme called *The Magic & Mystery Show* asked if they could film my circle conducting a séance I was delighted. This time I could demonstrate mediumship on my own territory and surrounded by the supporting vibrations of my circle members. We would have what Spiritualist call the 'right conditions'.

They used the same 14th century hall that I hold my weekly meetings, lowered the lights and tried to film discreetly as I conducted the séance. Next to me that sat the sceptical psychologist Dr Richard Wiseman and opposite me the presenter Nick Knowles who I was to give proof of life after death

I opened my circle in my usual way talking the group through opening the psychic centres and we entered the silence of meditation. The energy in the room began to build. I resisted trance but held myself on the brink as I gave a spirit message to Nick Knowles. As I linked in I could tell that Nick didn't know many people who had died but I felt someone draw close to me who was really close to him. "There's a young man you know in the spirit" I said "He liked motorcycles"

"Yes" replied Nick as Dr Wiseman sat next to me scribbling notes.

"He tells me that he died in Australia and that his name is ***** *****" Nick Knowles nearly fell off his seat as I gave him the first name and surname of his friend who's grave he specially visited in Australia. "He says that he was recently engaged to a girl called ******* before he died. Her birthday is **th ****. He sends his love and talks about children by the names of ***** and *****. You will be going to America soon."

Everything I had said was 100% except Nick hadn't made plans yet to visit America. I wasn't going to give them a chance to edit out the important bits so I shut up and told them that the power had now left me. I had learnt by now that TV will always edit what you say down to about 3 to 4 minutes at the most. They had to use what I'd said or cut it all.

All Richard Wiseman could argue was that if mediums get something wrong they say "Oh well that must be something for the future". But I'd only put America in the future and there was no way I could have cheated. I also had no idea who Nick Knowles was until they arrived and apparently they only decided to use him at the last minute. Also the spirit communicator wasn't of the Knowles family so he wouldn't have appeared in Nick's family tree. It was impossible for Dr Richard Wiseman to explain away how I knew these names and facts. I'd got em.

But the programme nearly didn't get transmitted at all.

They told me that what I'd said was so accurate that it may upset surviving relatives of Nick's dead friend. More likely they couldn't clear it with the ITC I thought. In order to show my section the programme was moved to late night viewing and they used a bleep to blank out the names and facts when I spoke to Nick. Fortunately however a commentator's voice explained that I'd given correct Christian names, surnames, locations and dates during my reading. But it wasn't quite the same.

I met Nick again sometime later when I was invited to do a telepathy experiment for a show called *Put it to the Test* with Carol Valderman. Nick admitted that he'd been extremely sceptical at first but what I had said on *The Magic & Mystery Show* had astonished him. I blew his socks off again when I did the telepathy test and described in accurate detail what was happening in a clip of film that was being shown only to the studio audience. There was absolutely no cheating and a member of staff sat with me in the green room to ensure that there was no way I could inadvertently overhear conversations about what they intended to do. The film showed a scrap car race with some cars in flames which I described as 'I feel confined like I am in a roller coaster but there are cars and flames flying. Whatever it is I am moving very fast. It's dangerous but exciting' I did a similar and successful telepathy with an audience for another regional show called the *Workhouse* for Anglia TV.

Our biggest TV triumph came when London Weekend Television approached us about making a programme. The producer Peter Davy told us that they had seen my first book *The Psychic Workbook (Vermilion)* and felt that some of the ideas in it would make a super TV programme.

The show would pit us and other psychics, astrologers and clairvoyants against pundits like Simon Hoggart, Angus 'Statto' Loughran and the *Daily Mail's* own Nigel Dempster to see who would make the more accurate predictions. Our answers to a range of questions about the future would be locked in a secret vault for six months and unveiled on the show. Hosted by

Phillip Schofield, this programme would be shown at peak time, after the lottery, on a Saturday evening and would reach a mass audience.

In the January they filmed us making our predictions at the exclusive Hemple Hotel that was founded by a London socialite. The exclusive Hemple Hotel is a favourite haunt of many big stars and is often visited by Michael Jackson. It's a weird place and in my opinion very pretentious.

Outside it just looks like an ordinary small terraced house. There's no signs or anything to indicate that it's a hotel. Instead men (or should I say male icons) dressed entirely black look out for expected guests arriving in their limousines. As you come the front door you are immediately faced with a plain white wall which you move behind to enter the gigantic reception area. This is a huge white room with no furniture or windows. The floors are made entirely from white marble and through the centre of the room runs a long trench of white coals from which rise gentle flames. At the far end is a big white marble slab behind which sits a black clad receptionist. She was completely dwarfed against the whiteness of everything around her. A thought flashed through my head "Did I pack the embalming fluid?" It would be quite easy to mistake this hotel for a mausoleum.

Of course the hotel is based upon abstract art and in particular the ideas enthroned in Minimalism the movement that gave us such great works as piles of bricks or blank canvases. In my opinion this was art with a capital F. We'd have been much more pleased if LWT had spent the money on something useful- such as our fee.

Six months later in June the vaults were unlocked and the predictions we filmed at the hotel were compared to what had happened in reality. By the time it came to the show at the studio and Phillip Schoefield walked onto the set to reveal our results we had forgotten what things we had said to camera six months ago. I know my heart was pounding and so must have Jane's as they replayed the film we had made six months earlier. Would the journalists shame us? We'd got a few very minor things wrong but overall we scored a resounding success with many direct hits. The astrologers and other psychics who took part also did very well but Nigel Dempster and his team of pundits were right with many of the general trends but way out when it came to the specifics.

Jane's hits for 97 included: Michael Jackson will have a baby son, Mary Allwood pregnant, Liam Gallegher to marry Patsie Kensit, David Janson to win a Bafta Award, Victoria from the Spice girls will get married. And some of mine included: Pamela Anderson treated by psychologists for depression, England to win 2-0 to Georgia a car hit by a small meteorite. We also filmed many other predictions which came true but edited out because of time including floods in Bangladesh, palace grounds breached, Serbian leadership falls and riots in Hong Kong- all of which came to pass.

Unfortunately television is looking for entertainment so the real message that we are trying to convey gets lost amongst the glitter and glamour of showbiz. Our mentor, Doris Stokes knew this and made sure people understood the difference between a psychic and a mediumistic powers. She made it plain that she couldn't tell the future. She could of course but by saying this it made the produces and public focus on the real message of her work which is that the human personality survives death. Predicting the football results and whatever could be left to the astrologers and card readers. She was absolutely right and I have learnt how television can turn profound philosophy into cheap titillating entertainment.

I was pleased when Channel 5 rang me up to ask if I'd appear on their 'Expresso' programme and demonstrate my mediumistic powers. The person I was to give a reading to on air was Ellen Jameson who is best known for co-hosting a Radio 2 show with husband Derek. To her astonishment and mine as well I suddenly felt Doris Stokes with me:

'Craig knew nothing about my link with Doris, but he came through to me on the show' Ellen told the Daily Mirror reported who wrote a feature about what happened. 'Craig said that Doris was telling him that the first words she ever said to you were "I'm not a Tarot reader you know". I remember the first thing Doris ever said to me was "Stop doing the tarot cards", and I nearly jumped out of my skin. I was dabbling with them because I'd recently lost my Mum and I was in turmoil. I suppose I was desperate and I'd always been interested in finding out more about the psychic world. We had a sitting together and Doris helped me actually "see" my Mum and hold a conversation with her. We talked about a dancing clown musical box I've had since I was a child that plays the tune Send In The Clowns. Mum was trying to cheer me up, and, over the years the music box has started up several times of its own accord whenever I've been feeling tearful.

'Craig also said that Doris was saying "You're a chocaholic but you're doing well". I was astounded because nobody knew I had battled to give up chocolate two years earlier. Craig also went on to say that I was in the process of painting my living room in a shocking shade of fuchsia which was also correct.

'He then said that Doris had "opened the door" and let my father through, and gave an amazingly accurate description of him. He described Dad as a small man who'd had trouble with his legs before he died, and said that he was quite foggy when he passed over. That was spot on and I was very moved.

'I don't know how I would cope with the loss of a loved one without my trust in mediums. It would seem very strange not to be able to contact the other side.'

It was wonderful to communicate with Doris when I was with Ellen. It was clear the two of them are very close and Doris wanted to comfort Ellen by passing on news of her father. It's wonderful when the spirits can help us in this life, and I think you are a very lucky person if you have a friend in the spirit world.

As you can see Jane and I have come a long way since my business collapsed and what you've read is only a small part of the many shows we've been on. They loved us when we went on the Gay Burns show in Ireland and I've recently had the Japanese asking questions about our work. I now have regular columns in newspapers all over the world and often write features for top publications such as The Daily Mail, Sunday Mirror, the People, The Record, Best magazine etc. etc. In more recent years we have had our own television series in the UK and many shows and TV series in the USA including a live worldwide TV broadcast to make contact with the spirit of Princess Diana.

There's were times when it seemed that all was lost but I'm sure that someone upstairs has been looking after us. If we hadn't experienced the bad times we'd have never have appreciated the good.

2 YOUR MIND READING POWERS

It can happen between lovers, friends, family or even with a pet. Telepathy is a mind to mind communication that has been with us before language was invented. Even today the aborigines of Australia still use this Stone Age skill to communicate with each other over great distances. Many hunting tribes in Africa and South America 'call' the animals to the hunt using mental powers. For example, tuna fishermen still entice the fish into their nets by mental command and to this day the chief shaman of the Gilbert Islands has the hereditary title of "porpoise caller". His duty, which he enacts at auspicious festival times, is to call the dolphins by telepathy.

Most people are, to some degree, telepathic but they either pay little attention to it, or don't even realise that they're displaying anything remarkable. If you finish people's sentences for them or say the same thing at the same time you may be displaying these mind reading skills. Have you ever realised who's calling even before you answer the phone? This experience is very common and you may notice that it will happen mostly when friends or family ring but not if the call is from a stranger or salesman. This is because the powers of telepathy work best between people who like each other or, better still, love each other. Tests in the laboratory indicate that this is true and if it happens to you it's a good sign that a friendship or relationship is on the right track.

This telepathic bonding may have a survival function associated with falling in love and choosing the right mate. Once a strong telepathic bonding has been established the information communicated between the individuals increases beyond the feeling level to include shared imagery and thoughts.

The fact is that you probably already have these telepathic powers and with a little help and development, they could assist you in your life. Soon you can try my specially devised tests to see the extent of the powers **you** possess. Telepathy is a Greek word. "Tele" means 'from a distance' and "Pathy" means 'to feel'. It is a perfectly natural skill that has been neglected and now lies dormant within the mind.

Just as telepathy traditionally happens between members of a tribe so we see telepathy at work in our own modern society. These ancient skills are active at work, in the home, between lovers in fact in all areas of life. The fact is most people are unaware that it's happening at all. However, if you scrutinise some of the events in your life you may find that telepathy is happening more often than you thought. In the following sections are revealed the secret workings of telepathy that influences you in mysterious ways that you may never have thought possible......

TELEPATHY AT WORK

In pre-language societies teamwork would have been very important particularly at dangerous times such as the hunt or during tribal wars. A group of hunters would need to be aware of each other's position in relation to the quarry and would need to be able to anticipate each other's moves. Sometimes the chase would take place over many miles and it would have been very difficult to liaise with each other. In these situations humans with a telepathic ability would have had the evolutionary edge.

The modern workplace is like a hunt- except nowadays it's profit rather than prey we seek. Team building has been recognised as essential and modern management jargon includes military and hunting terminology- i.e. targets, strategy, objectives, etc. Even in the stock market they use terms such as bull, bear and stag markets. Given that telepathy is active during the hunt, it's not surprising that it can often play a role in the modern workplace.

Psychic researcher Betty Humphrey from Duke University, USA discovered that extrovert personalities displayed better telepathy than introverts. Consequently the extrovert salesman or manager is more likely to be receptive to, and able to project telepathy. For example, telepathic people will trust their gut feeling when employing a new member of staff or establishing a business partnership. So if it's you in the hot seat looking for work project good thoughts towards your would be employer. Their unconscious may respond to your telepathic signals and instinctively they will be more likely to trust you.

The evil Russian monk Rasputin is said to have had hypnotic powers that he could project telepathically. During the Cold War both the Russians and CIA employed telepaths to 'remote influence' enemy world leaders. These telepathic powers of persuasion may be used unconsciously by the commanding businessman. A study made in America suggests that telepathic people are often more successful in business and make better leaders.

It has also been established that gamblers and risk takers display higher than average telepathic abilities and score above chance in telepathy card guessing tests. The archetypal risk taking entrepreneur is likely to be unconsciously using these skills for his day to day decisions. For example a hunch about the stock market may be triggered by their perception of collective thoughts being transmitted by people at financial markets around the world.

But it is imaginative, creative people, and particularly artists, who score best in telepathy tests. Some researchers believe that this is because telepathic people predominately use the right-hand side of the brain- the side that's responsible for intuition. Some of the most influential businessmen and politicians started their careers from creative media and advertising backgrounds.

TIPS FOR BETTER TELEPATHY AT WORK:

1. Express the extrovert side of your personality.
2. Trust your gut feeling about people and business hunches.
3. Realise that your own thoughts can directly influence others.
4. Try to be creative with your thinking.

TELEPATHY AND RELATIONSHIPS

Your most startling experiences of telepathy may have taken place when you were in love. Lovers naturally share thoughts and are sometimes so in tune with each other that they finish each other's sentences or say the same thing at the same time. When they are parted they 'know' when their love is thinking of them or 'know' if they are feeling sad or worried. Lovers may buy each other the same presents or independently make the same plans. Science has already recognised that people in love copy each other's body language but there is now evidence to suggest that their brain patterns mimic each other as well. Lovers are literally on the same wavelength.

Laboratory experiments using card the guessing techniques first conceived by the American scientist Joseph Banks Rhine have shown that telepathic abilities appear to increase if the 'receiver' and 'sender' like each other. It has also been found that the friendliness scientists conducting the experiment may also effect the results. In short, people who trust each other and get on well can telepathically communicate with each other more easily than those who don't like one another. This is amplified even more when we are in love.

There is evidence to suggest that lovers who say that they know what their partner is feeling at a given time may be experiencing telepathy over a distance. It has been found that telepathy appears to take place over any distance. One of the most famous experiments in distant telepathic communication was conducted in 1971 by Edgar Mitchell aboard the Apollo 14 moon mission. In these secret experiments Mitchell beamed images to a 'receiver' on earth.

The telepathic bonding between lovers has been recognised throughout history. The Tantric sexual yoga texts from India and Tibet say that telepathic powers are triggered by sexual energy. There is also mention of telepathic thought sharing in the Japanese and Chinese 'pillow books' such as the *Ishinpoo* And from India the infamous *Karma Sutra, Koka Shastra* and the *Ananga Raga* all link sexuality with paranormal powers of the mind.

Lovers are also more likely to believe in the telepathy that they spontaneously share and it will rightly be seen as a sign that the relationship is going well. Scientists say that people who believe in telepathic powers display higher abilities than those who don't. In short telepathy works best between people who believe in telepathic powers and who care for each other.

TIPS FOR BETTER TELEPATHY BETWEEN PARTNERS:

- Recognise that the more you care for each other the more paranormal thoughts you'll share.
- Believe that your powers are real.
- Try ringing your partner at odd times to ask how they are feeling.
- Be aware of how often you say the same things at the same time.

TELEPATHY AT HOME

The family environment is the most likely place you will have your first telepathic experiences for here the powers of love are manifest between partners, children and even the pets. In particular telepathic bonding may be an important evolutionary function for the protection of the young.

Many young mothers say that they feel a telepathic link with their new-born babies and tests by psychologists have confirmed this. Experiments have shown that if a sleeping baby is put into a soundproof room, his mother's heartbeat will increase the moment he wakes up even though there's no way the mother could have actually heard his cries. Furthermore it has been suggested by the psychiatrist Jan Ehrenwald that telepathy is a pre-language survival aptitude and occurs between mother and infant during the dependent period before the child acquires language. Once verbal communication is mastered, telepathic communication is no longer fundamental to survival, and the ability is either suppressed or lost.

Fathers also can have a telepathic bonding with their children. It is a popular misconception that women are more psychic than men but laboratory tests show that they have equal telepathic powers. However women are much more likely to talk about their experiences and 85% of people who report paranormal events are women.

Within the home telepathic thoughts are being shared all the time. Perhaps you've noticed how moods, both good and bad, are almost infectious in the home. One of the children starts to play up and soon everybody is upset. OK this is mainly due to normal human reactions but have you noticed how more intuitively sensitive you are to your family's moods and feelings? Laboratory tests undertaken at Edinburgh University have demonstrated that moods, feelings, and emotions are easier to communicate by telepathy than words, pictures or numbers.

In a happy home even the pets and plants may respond to the thoughts vibrating around the house. Rupert Shelldrake is currently accumulating a wealth of evidence to suggest that pets respond to their owners thoughts. For example they may know when their owner is coming home or even obey mental commands you send then. And perhaps the strangest effect of telepathy will be seen in your household plants. In the 1960's Cleve Baxter showed that plants wired to a lie detector will respond to mental thoughts projected at it. Happy thoughts make plants grow whereas hateful thoughts make them wilt.

Given that telepathy is at work within the home you may be able to tell if it's a happy place by the state of the plants.

TIPS FOR BETTER TELEPATHY AT HOME:

1. Try to guess what mood your partner is in before to come home.

2. See if your children will respond to your mental commands i.e. think about sweets and see if they ask you for some

3. Remember that telepathy works best on an emotional level- notice how your moods unconsciously effect other people.

4. Observe the family pet- does the dog wait for you at the window when you return home?

TELEPATHY FOR PROTECTION

Have you ever been aware that someone is staring at you? Again this may be another situation where telepathy is at work. Some interesting results are coming out of the labs in recent years that indicate that many people know when they are being stared at. A typical 'remote staring' experiment involves situating the participant in a shielded chamber while someone else stares at them via a closed circuit video. The pulse, and physiological and psychological responses are then monitored to see whether the person is aware of when they are being watched. Establishments such as the Koestler Chair of Parapsychology at Edinburgh University, the University of Utrecht and Duke University and the University of Nevada in the USA are establishing a body of evidence to scientifically prove the reality of telepathy.

It would be very useful when mankind lived in the wild to know if a predator was stalking him. You are experiencing these ancient instincts when you unconsciously realise that you are being watched. You may draw on these same powers when, for no apparent reason, you feel uncomfortable or threatened by certain people. It is likely that you are sensing that they may mean you harm. Even with our day to day contact with people your gut feeling is based upon the telepathic impressions you are unconsciously receiving.

It has been found that telepathically gifted people are usually cheerful and sensitive. You may find that your moods are easily affected by the people around you. If you are like this then its important to trust these impressions you are receiving.

Finally telepathy can come in very useful at times of crisis. Many people have spoken to me about how they've known that someone they love is in danger or have altered their plans because the correctly sensed that someone meant them harm. I was personally involved in a minor car accident and my wife knew what had happened as soon as I walked through the front door. Telepathic thoughts are floating all around us all the time like radio signals that we can tune in to. They can give us warnings, insight, express our feelings and even protect us.

TIPS FOR BETTER TELEPATHY IN A CRISIS:

- Trust your first impressions- your telepathic powers may be warning you that a person is not trustworthy..
- Record your dreams- they can often contain telepathically transmitted information from people far away. Check if you and your friends have ever shared a dream.
- Be happy- telepathy works best with cheerful people.
- Stare at someone- see if they react and realise they are being watched.

NOW TEST YOUR MIND READING POWERS

Simply answer yes or no to the following questions to find out if you're telepathic:

1. Are you bright, bubbly and perhaps like being the centre of attention at parties?

2. Do you take risks with money, career and love and may even enjoy the thrill of a bet?

3. Are you very sensitive and get easily hurt by what people say to you?

4. Are you creative? Perhaps you like to paint, write or play music and always have imaginative ideas?

5. Do you believe that psychic powers are absolutely real and that sceptics are frightened by what will one day be proved by science?

6. Are you so sceptical that you believe that if tested for telepathy you'd score well below chance?

7. Have you ever worried that someone you know at another location is in danger and it was later proved to be true?

8. Are you intuitive? Maybe you judge people by first impressions to find out later that you initial gut instinct was correct?

9. Do you sometimes know who's calling before you answer the phone?

10. Do pets respond to your feelings or know when you're coming home?

YOUR ANSWERS

Score 3 points for every 'yes' and 2 for every 'no' then add them up.

1. Psychic researcher Betty Humphrey from Duke University, USA discovered that extrovert personalities displayed better telepathy abilities than introverts.

2. It has been shown that gamblers and risk takers display higher than average telepathic abilities and score above chance in telepathy card guessing tests.

3. A telepathic person's mood is easily influenced by the thoughts and emotions of people around them. They can sometimes feel vulnerable and may experience mood changes.

4. Imaginative, creative people, and particularly artists, score better in telepathy tests than systematic thinkers. Some researchers believe that this is because telepathic people predominantly use the right-hand side of the brain- the side that's responsible for intuition.

5. People who believe in extra sensory perception (ESP) often score better in telepathy tests than sceptics. However, some sceptics have telepathic abilities whether they like it or not and score significantly below chance in card tests. If no telepathy were involved they would have only achieve a chance score.

6. Some sceptics have telepathic abilities whether they like it or not and score significantly below chance in card tests. If no telepathy were involved they would have only achieve a chance score.

7. Experiments reveal that telepathy appears to work over any distance. In 1971 secret telepathy experiments were carried out aboard the Apollo 14 moon mission by Edgar D Mitchell who mentally beamed images to a 'receiver' on earth.

8. Much of the information we get through intuition is gained by telepathy. If you finish people's sentences for them, you may be picking up their thoughts. Women trust their intuition more than men: 85 per cent of people who report paranormal events are women.

9. This is one of the most commonly reported experiences of telepathy. Sometimes people who haven't spoken to each other in years try to phone each other at exactly the same time.

10. Many people have a telepathic affinity with animals and a body of evidence is being accumulated by Rupert Sheldrake to suggest that some pets really do know when their owner is coming home.

How did you score?

20-23 Your scull is like a wall of stone. There's no way telepathic thoughts can get in and out of your head.

24-27 Not bad. You could improve your telepathic powers with a little thought.

28-30 Liars beware- you can read people like a book.

A PARTY TELEPATHY EXPERIMENT TO TRY.

Parapsychologists have found that to get a high score in telepathic tests it's important to be in a cheerful frame of mind as this somehow increases people's ability to communicate by thought. And get the kids involved as well because children are often more telepathic than adults. There's nothing demeaning about doing telepathy experiments in a party atmosphere- in fact you will probably get better results than in the top labs.

Here's what to do: Write down the list of subjects printed below on scraps of paper, fold them up and put them in a bag. Now one person is blindfolded and sits on a chair in the middle of the room. One of the subjects is chosen at random from the bag and passed around so that everyone except the 'receiver' who is blindfolded know what it is. The 'receiver' then expresses the feelings and thoughts that they have about the target subject.

SENDERS: The 'senders, must try to get as emotionally involved in the subject as possible and try to involve all of the five senses when they transmit their thoughts. For example, supposing you chose the topic 'Burning your fingers on a coal fire'. You must feel the pain, see the reds and oranges of the fire, feel the movement of the flames, hear the crackling and smell the smoke.

RECEIVER: The 'receiver' must deeply relax and let their mind become as still as possible. Don't struggle to guess what the image is, instead let your thoughts flow and immediately say whatever comes into your head no matter how silly it may sound. You must be completely spontaneous with what you say or your own mind will interfere with the telepathic impressions you receive.

Afterwards count up how many of the things said come close to the target response and how many were wrong. You'll probably find that the answers you get are more accurate than could ever be achieved by guesswork alone.

SOME TARGET SUBJECTS: (Of course you can make up your own as well.) 1. A coal burning your fingers, 2. A wet dog barking. 3. Falling out of an aeroplane without a parachute. 4. Running through a forest. 5. Biting into a lemon. 6. Walking through the snowy mountains. 7. Water skiing. 8. Riding a bicycle. 9. Dancing at a rock concert. 10. Running though the waves by an exotic beach.

TELEPATHY CASEBOOKS:

TELEPATHY PREVENTED MY MURDER

Joan Scowcroft was having breakfast in a restaurant at the quiet village of Holemoor in North Devon when a very odd looking man came through the door. "His behaviour, posture and facial expression all indicated that he was 'not quite right'. Then he lurched towards me and grabbed my keys. He dashed out of the restaurant and made off towards town."

Fortunately, Joan was immediately able to ring the police and by lunch time the keys were back in her possession. The police cautioned the man and ordered him to stay away from the village. Joan, a little shaken, returned home to her cottage. "Despite the police's reassurances I still felt ill at ease" says Joan "I kept seeing images in my mind's eye of the man stalking me. It was as if I could sense his thoughts reaching out to me like the feeling someone was staring at me. Suddenly I was gripped with fear. My cats began to make a pitiful whining sound. 'My God! He's coming to get me' I said out loud.

"I was feeling very nervous and to take my mind off my worries I decided to make some changes in the kitchen. To start with I decided to swap the kitchen knives, which included a dagger like instrument, from the draw and replace them with tea towels.

"No sooner had I finished when I heard a key turn in the lock and the next moment I was confronted by the madman. He strode into the kitchen and stood beside the draw that I had just emptied. 'The Lord has ordered me to kill you so that this cottage will become mine' he bellowed 'I will make it as quick and clean as I can.'

"As he spoke, his eyes fixed on me, he opened the draw........ and felt the tea towels.

"The next moment he shrieked a string of blasphemy and sacrilege, swore he would never work for the Lord again, and raced from the cottage

"I believe the if I and my cats hadn't telepathically pre-empted the madman's intentions, I'd be dead by now"

The police investigation that followed revealed that the man had got another set of keys cut during the short time they were in his possession. Unfortunately, he was never caught. Joan has sold her house and relocated to a new town.

My verdict: The way Joan describes her feelings is suggestive that telepathy is a work. She had a nagging feeling of fear and sensed that she's being watched. For many people their only experience of telepathy is during a crisis situation or when their lives are in danger. Even the cats knew something was wrong. This case demonstrates how Telepathy is an interracial part of our ancient survival skills.

TELEPATHY CASE 2:

DAD HELD ON FOR DEBORAH

"My labour pains started at 1 a.m. but I told my husband not to call my parents as they were probably experiencing a bad night." recalls Joan Lodge (67) from Melbury Osmond near Dorchester "My father was terminally ill and we were expecting him to pass over at any time. 'We'll let him know when it's all over' I remember saying."

Joan gave birth to her daughter at two minutes past three in the morning

"The next day my husband went to tell Mum and Dad- and was greeted by my Mum. 'I know' she said before my husband could speak 'we've got a granddaughter.'

"Apparently my father had been sleeping peacefully for once when he suddenly sat up in bed and shook my mother awake. 'Baby Deborah's coming!, She's coming! She's HERE! exclaimed dad.

"Mum looked at the clock. 2 minutes past 3 a.m."

"Its a funny way to choose a name" says Deborah, now 43 "Granddad held me in his arms just before he died. Mum keeps pointing out how similar I am to him apparently I have the same mannerisms and even his turns of phrase. He obviously loved me a great deal and sometimes I feel that in his spirit is somehow guiding me.

MY VERDICT: Distance seems to make no difference for telepathy to work. There was a telepathic empathy between Deborah and her granddad from the moment she was born and may still be happening between this world and the next.

TELEPATHY CASE 3

GRANDMOTHER HAD DAUGHTER'S BABY

"The excruciating pain started on my way to the shops in Badminton" says Bridgette Stafford from Acton Turville in Gloucester. "I found a seat and sat down. The pain seemed to come and go in waves and in this sorry state and sometimes writhing in agony I managed to somehow struggle home

"Of course I was worried that there was something seriously wrong with me. As I came through the front door of my home it seemed to be getting worse and worse. I slumped exhausted into an arm chair and was about to reached for the phone to call the doctor when I was overwhelmed with a great spasm of pain.

"It was so bad that I called out.

Unbeknown to Bridgette her daughter Nicola was at that same moment was in hospital and having a very difficult birth. "The baby kept crowning and going back" says Nicola (39) "The only option left was a forceps delivery. I had lots of Pethidine but the pain was more than I could take. Suddenly I found myself on the ceiling and looking down at everything that was going on. Then the baby came and the next thing I knew was back in bed holding her in my arms"

At the same time Bridgette felt the pain lift from her too. "All of a sudden I felt completely at peace. All the pain had gone as quickly and as unexpectedly as it had started. I felt fine and desperately wanted a cup of tea. At that moment the phone rang. It was my daughter ringing from the hospital 'Congratulations Nan,' said Nicola in an excited voice, 'You're the first to know. I've was rushed in and have just had baby Kristina a just few minutes ago'

"I'm sure that I shared my daughter's labour pains that day and may have experienced even more pain than she did! I now have 9 grandchildren but I'm very close to Kristina. It's always me she calls for if she's ill and I always seem to know if she's troubled"

Nicola often wonders if her mother had somehow shared in Kristina's difficult birth. "We sometimes laugh about it now" says Nicola "When I was out of my body it was like I said 'The pain's too much. Here Mum - you have it!'"

MY VERDICT: Scientific experiments may prove that there is a mysterious link between mother and baby. This same telepathic empathy exists between people who care for each other. Nicola's thoughts reached out and linked with her mum.

TELEPATHY IS AN ANCIENT BUT FORGOTTEN SKILL

I have suggested at the beginning of this chapter that telepathy and ESP are and ancient survival skill that everybody may have possessed in the times before language. It's not surprising therefore to discover that animals and our pets are also psychic.

Barbra Woodhouse, the famous TV animal trainer, was convinced that mind to mind communication (telepathy) takes place between humans and pets. "I have always been able to understand and read their thoughts" she said "They come on my brain just as if they were speaking my language. It is what we send out to them that matters. It goes out in waves. I feel the waves coming back."

She didn't realise that her telepathic gifts were unusual "I thought everyone could do it" she said at a literary luncheon "I was quite surprised when I found people did not hear what their dogs were thinking."

Many pet owners believe exactly the same. "I have a Siamese cat called

'Biscuits' and I'm sure that he's psychic." says Jenny Ashwell a vet's secretary from Dibden near Southampton, "He miraculously appears at the doorstep the moment I arrive home from work. Even when I arrive early or late he still seems to know when I'll arrive. My son Airrion, who lives with me, has noticed that Biscuits will jump up on the windowsill and look for me if I telephone to say I'm on my way home."

I've noticed similar behaviour in our family Jack Russell dog William and our rabbits Charley and Benjamin seem to obey our mental commands if we will them out from the back garden and in through the back door.

William escaped from the garden one day when my wife Jane was out visiting a friend's new house three miles away. "I was amazed when William turned up at my friend's" says Jane "I'd travelled by car, so there is no way I could have left a scent, and William had never been taken to that address before."

One of the most strange stories of pets finding their masters happened to Private James Brown of the 1st North Staffordshire Regiment when he was sent to join the Great War in France in August 1914. On the 27th September, his wife wrote to him to break the bad news that Prince, his Irish terrier, was missing. But Prince had already joined his master in the trenches. The dog had somehow travelled over 200 miles through the South of England, crossed the English Channel and then walked another 60 miles of battlefield to his master's front line position at Armentieres.

Scientific research is slowly beginning to substantiate the many anecdotal claims of pet owners who say that their animals are psychic. Psychologist Michael Fox of Washington University studied extraordinary cases of psychic cats. For example he records, a New York vet who left his pet behind when he was relocated to a new job 2,500 miles away in California. Six months later an identical cat walked into his new home. When he examined it he found a deformation on the fourth vertebra of the tail- an injury he had himself treated when the cat was bitten as a kitten.

Animals who find their owners in this way may be displaying a form of clairvoyance that parapsychologists have called 'remote viewing'. This is the ability to 'see' distant locations without the use of the five senses. During the Cold War the CIA funded psychics to use this technique to spy on Soviet military bases.

In Russia the Soviets had their own X-Files and much of their paranormal research was done with animals. According to Dr Pavel Naumov a series of shockingly cruel tests were undertaken with rabbits to see if telepathy (mind-to-mind communication) took place between a mother rabbit and her new born litter. A submarine was commandeered, the baby rabbits taken on board, and the mother rabbit wired up on shore with electrodes to monitor her brain patterns. The baby rabbits were then killed at pre arranged times and the mother rabbits brain waves tested. "At the instant of death, her brain reacted" says Dr Naumov "There *was* communication and our instruments clearly registered these moments of ESP."

French scientific experiments showed that rats randomly selected to die would react *beforehand* demonstrating that animals also have the ability to foresee the future.

Today's scientists, such as Rupert Sheldrake, say that living things have morphogenic fields- invisible vibrations that surround and give shape to life forms, and affect their behaviour. This interconnection of life energy and thought extends across the barriers between species and may even increase the intelligence of animals as a result of contact with their human companions.

Pets have often been known to mimic human behaviour and can sometimes display remarkably intelligent actions. For example they frequently learn to cope with door fasteners of new refrigerators so that they can help themselves to food, within minutes of the refrigerators installation. Parapsychologists have argued that they receive this information from the thoughts of their owners.

And just we influence our pets so they in turn influence us. Tests with patients suffering from high blood pressure reveal that both systolic and diastolic blood pressure will reduce when a pet is present. Research in America shows that pet owning cardiac patients live longer than other patients with similar heart conditions.

The father of parapsychology, J B Rhine, dedicated his life to the study of ESP (Extra Sensory Perception) and psychic phenomena. He wrote "The number of reported cases on animal ESP is large enough to suggest that animals can somehow be affected by circumstances they could not be aware of by any sensory sign and which one would suppose they could hardly understand in human terms"

In other words: animals are psychic!

3 DÉJÀ VU AND PSYCHIC TIME TRAVEL

Most people have experienced that eyrie feeling of déjà vu which literally means 'seen before'. For example, part-way through a conversation everything that's being said seems strangely familiar. It's like watching a movie then suddenly realising that you've already seen it. Except this is real life. You've feel that lived these moments once before. It's all happening again....

This is a classic example of déjà vu, in which a person feels that they have witnessed or experienced a situation before. Usually the sensation lasts only a few seconds but there are pathological cases on record where the subject has prolonged or even a constant feeling of déjà vu. The phenomena is experienced occasionally by the majority of normal people usually under conditions of fatigue or heightened sensitivity.

Science still can't adequately explain it. One theory says that it is caused when one side of the brain receives messages a fraction of a second after the other. Or it may be that the déjà vu experience is a memory mix up caused when repressed memories surface. Some say that is simply that the experience reminds you of real part-recalled events- like the infuriating act of trying to recall a name that's on the tip of your tongue.

But how does science explain-away the experiences of people such as David Martin from Southsea in Portsmouth who told me about his déjà vu experience in Singapore? Whilst travelling through some unfamiliar terrain in a jeep with his friends he had a profound sense of déjà vu and soon realised that he 'knew' the unfamiliar terrain "At the cross-roads I said 'Turn left here because just down the road is a lovely tea house. It has a large red sign and a large stone dog outside. When we approach a Malaysian girl dressed in black will wave to us.'

"Everyone in the car laughed and reminded me that none of us had ever visited the area before. We turned left and there was the tea house exactly as I described it with the, red sign, stone dog and the Malaysian girl stood outside waving to us."

David's déjà vu, like thousands of similar reports, includes information about the future- a future that was to unfold only moments after he had made his prediction.

Similarly many people have told me how they've seen back through time and witness events from the past. These spontaneous uncalled for glimpses may explain some of the strange and consistent accounts of ghostly sightings.

For example, John Slade and his wife Elsie from Petersfield spoke of their strange experience in Sri Lanka. "To get to our hotel in time we were forced to cut across the railway line" says John. "The old steam trains normally made quite a racket- you could hear them hissing and clanking from miles away. I noticed a bright light behind us. Assuming that a train was coming I quickly pulled my wife away from the rails as a large train brushed by, almost touching us.

"Even though it was an old steam train it was totally silent- not just quiet, it was *totally* silent. The steam, the wheels, the carriages made not a single sound. We were so close that we could also see that the train had no driver, no passengers and no guard.

"I'm a sceptical man- I was trained in the navy and have worked as a councillor- so I went next morning to ask the stationmaster about the incident. He insisted that no trains passed that way at the times I said. And he added that the track where we not the first to see this strange train. Where we had walked had been the site of a number of fatal train disasters!"

John and Elsie believed that they had seen a ghost train. Or did they experience a time slip and witness a scene from the past?

I have been sent so many of these convincing, strange stories that I'm beginning to believe that popular television programmes such as *Goodnight Sweetheart* no longer as daft as they seem. Is it possible for ordinary people, who make no claim to psychic powers, to 'see' both the past and future?

Psychologist Dr Keith Herne is a member of the Society for Psychical Research and heads the BBC's prediction bureaux for the programme *Out of this World*. "Premonition exists- even though it defies the known laws of the universe." says the eminent scientist, "Everything in the universe may happen all at once and our lifetime is but one segment of this wholeness. I predict that one of the most important questions for the science of the next millennium will be concerned with the illusion of time."

It could be that precognition is an ancient instinctive warning signal and this may explain why it's the threatening events ahead that are the most easily perceived. And for some people unwanted visions of the future can be very worrying. "I kept having terrible repetitive nightmares of a nuclear disaster by a tall tower" says Mrs Feist of Winchester "I would thrash in my sleep and was heard to call out 'The Russians! The Russians!'

"The meaning of my nightmares was revealed on the television some weeks later. I saw on the News a picture of the very tower that I had just been dreaming about: The Chernobyl power station in Russia."

But one of the most chilling stories of precognition was sent to me by Mr Lizakowski from Shipley in West Yorkshire. "In the early 1960's I attended Cottingley Manor School and I remember how a schoolboy was describing a dream in the school playground to every boy or girl present there. 'Peter will commit murder' he said convincingly. 'And it will be horrible! horrible! horrible!' In distressed tones he said the words over and over again."

Nobody believed the boy's terrible prophesy about their classmate- Peter Sutcliffe.

CAN YOU SEE THROUGH TIME?

Over the years I have trained many people to unlock their powers of prophesy. At first my students believe that they have no special powers but with a little practice they quickly obtain sometimes quite startling results.

The most important key to predictive power is to BELIEVE IN YOURSELF! Trust your intuitive insight. Don't censor your thoughts. Allow your intuition to tell you what it already knows. You can see through time and soon you're going to prove it.

The truth is, you already have the power to look into time. But you are unaware of it. With a little help and some deliberate experimentation you will see how easy it is to trigger these extraordinary powers.

First, you need to ask yourself the specially devised questions printed opposite. If you can answer yes to most or all of them you are already a long way down the path to seership. Afterwards try the simple experiments printed at the bottom of this page to test just how accurate your powers to see through time are.

THE POWER OF PROPHESY?

Simply answer yes or no to the following questions:

- Have you ever dreamed of a future event and it's happened?
- When visiting a strange place have you had a sense that you've been there before?
- Have you applied for a job and just known you're going to get it even though the odds were stacked against you?
- Have you known, despite their abilities, that some childhood friends would do well in life and others fail?
- Do you ever know what somebody's going to wear before you meet them?
- Have you ever cancelled a journey because of a gut feeling that something bad was going to happen?
- When playing card games have you ever anticipated which card will be drawn next?
- Have the News Headlines ever reflected your own misgivings about what will happen?
- Are you lucky with the National Lottery?
- Have you ever felt that a friend will unexpectedly get into trouble and they do?

HOW DID YOU SCORE?

- If you answered no to every question, you've got a long way to go before being able to see the future. In fact, you may never experience precognitive thoughts because you're resisting them.
- If you answered yes to one to four questions, you have an average precognition ability. Given time, you could develop it.
- If your score was between five and eight, you really do have a gift.

Your mind is definitely receptive to future events.
- Between eight and 10? You're a regular Madam Za Za and can see the future- but then you probably know that already!

Can you 'see' the past?

Many psychics and mediums believe that a stream of vibration emanates from everyone and is absorbed into the environment. When you visit an ancient building such as a cathedral you may become aware of these vibrations and sense this as an 'atmosphere'. You can *feel* the holiness and peace of the place in your bones.

Most people employ this sensitivity to the past when they buy a home. A place has to 'feel right' before you buy it. A 'gut' feeling tells you whether it 'feels like home' or has a 'horrible atmosphere'. You are reading the vibrations of good or ill that once occurred in that place.

In the same way vibrations can be absorbed into objects like jewellery or a watch and can unlocked by a psychic technique called psychometry. An object held in the hand contains the whole history of events that once took place around it.

Here's an experiment to try:

1. Ask a friend to lend you a small object such as a watch or ring, belonging to someone they know. The history of the object should be known by your friend but unknown to you. You're going to describe the life and character of the object's owner.

2. Close your eyes, relax and allow your intuitive thinking to flow. Believe in yourself- don't worry about making mistakes. Say exactly what comes to you and don't censor or interpret the images that you see. What is the first thing you feel? Is this a warm person or a cold, insensitive person? Is this person a worrier? Are they happy or sad? Shy or out going?

3. Now dig deeper. Describe any scenes and pictures that come to mind. Can you describe their childhood. What significant events have happened in their life. What countries have they visited? Do any other locations come to mind? In short describe a short history of their life. Let it flow. But don't make predictions. Psychometry is all about reading the past.

5. When you dry up, ask your friend to tell you what percentage you got right. Ask them also about specific things you may have said. Psychometry

is a psychic ability that most people can develop with practice and you may really surprise yourself with your accuracy!

RETRO-COGNITION

Many ordinary people claim to have had spontaneous glimpses of the past. For some it is more than sensing an atmosphere, they see a whole series of events unfold just as if they are experiencing these things first hand. It may be that they glimpse into some other level of reality that is beyond time and space as we understand it. When I suggested that people write to my newspapers columns about their glimpses of history I was surprised not only at the size of my mailbag but the amazing vividness of the experiences described. The casebooks that follow have had to be abridged but the detail reveals more about the writers' reactions. Often they are puzzled or frightened by what happened and its clear that these bizarre stories are not made up. Something certainly happened but I'll leave it up to you to decide if these people really are time travellers or just tricked somehow by their unconscious. The scale of the response to my request makes me marvel at just how commonplace these glimpses of history are. There's an awful lot of time travellers out there.

Here's a few fascinating examples from people who've written to me together with my comments in reply that explain what's happened to them:

'"I've just seen a lovely dinner service on a stand near the shop over there" said my husband as we looked around the local market' says Beverley from Portsmouth. '"If we're quick we may just be able to buy it in time." As we rushed over to the stall, he told me that a strange old lady with long grey hair tied back ran it. The stall had the oddest collection of things for sale- most of them from the 1950's.

'But when we got to the stall it was completely empty. Only seconds ago it had been full of wares. Perplexed by what had happened, my husband asked a man, who was sat nearby selling his paintings, if he had seen the old lady and her stall. "I couldn't understand why you were looking at an empty stall" said the man "And who were you talking to?"

'Further enquiries revealed that the site of the stall was once owned by a little old lady with distinctive long grey hair. She had stopped trading in the 1950's. Did my husband have a vision of the past?'

Beverley's case is typical of the letters sent me on this intriguing subject of looking into time. Of course Beverley may have seen a ghost but strikes me as more like a 'time slip' It sounds like science fiction but there are also many well authenticated examples. For example, some visitors to the palace of Versailles near Paris have suddenly found themselves transported to the time of Marie Antoinette. Remarkably, the scenes these psychic time travellers have described could be checked and proved to be historically accurate. The details described by them about the palace's layout are only known to the most knowledgeable historians.

Another explanation may be that these are not 'time slips' but unconscious memories of past lives. We'll come back to this subject in a chapter later. Meanwhile consider Len Rodney's story. Was this a time slip, clairvoyance, precognition or perhaps he'd once lived in Russia centuries ago? How would you react if this happened to you?:

'While sightseeing in Russia fourteen years ago, I came across a large ornamental monument in a public garden.' says Len Rodney from Manchester 'As soon as I set eyes on it I had a strange feeling that I had seen it before. I stood for some time before I remembered. I had dreamed about it , in every detail: The black and white marble squares, the little arched wooden door at the top flanked by two colourful dragons that spouted water from their mouths to the row of white marble statues on either side of the monument.

'In my dream I slid down the tiles and past the dragons. I wondered if I lived there in a past life and slid down those familiar banisters as a child? How on earth could I have dreamed in such detail of a place where I have never been before?'

Certain places give me an eyrie feeling as if I've known the place before but can't for the life of me explain when. Perhaps it's caused by dim memories of our past lives that are trying to awaken since we crossed the river of forgetting or maybe we are picking up vibrations left recorded in the environment. Whatever the explanation an experience of this sort can shake even the most courageous of men:

'While working for the Fire Brigade we were called to extinguish a fire at an old stone building that had long ago been used as a lodging house.' says Harry MacMillan from Edinburgh in Scotland. 'When we returned to the station we realised that we had left behind a shovel so I returned alone to get it.

'As I stood in the silent, smouldering building I noticed an old wooden structure that must have been the serving area where the owner would have allocated the beds for the night. Suddenly I was transported back in time and actually saw the lines of flotsam and jetsam queuing up. I also heard many different dialects being spoken. Soon I became aware of the drudgery that these poor people lived with and sensed their presence all around me and felt a great sadness for these ghostly figures. The scene so engrossed me that I couldn't even remember picking up the shovel that was now in my hand. This vision of despair was so powerful that it has stayed with me all of my life. I believe that somehow I had seen through time and I still shudder when I think of it.'

Harry's experience reminds me of the well known story from the West Country. In 1936, a sixteen year old, named Stephen Jenkins was exploring in Loe Bar in Cornwall where King Arthur is said to have met his death. He was astonished to see a host of medieval warriors in chain mail appear before him. Thirty eight years later he returned to the same spot with his wife and the same vision reappeared to both of them.

Some people claim that places such as Loe Bar are situated on the intersection of Ley-lines and are places of great psychic power. Ley-lines are lines of natural energy that allegedly run through the earth and connect ancient monuments. Maybe the building the Harry McMillan visited was also a place of great psychic energy.

Many Scottish people have written to my columns and I'm convinced that they are a very special people with a unique psychic heritage that stretches back way before the times of the Celts. Many great mediums were Scots but also many of my best letters came from the ordinary folk of Scotland. One of my favourite casebook letters takes us back to the early history of wild Scotland when witches, elves and fairies roamed the land:

'In 1966 my wife and I decided to holiday at the Isle of Skye.' says Earnest Rowe from Glasgow. 'It was a late evening in August when we approached the bridge near Dunvegin. We came across a enormous number of cats. They were everywhere and there was even some jumping on to the bonnet of our van. I have never seen so many cats gathered together at one time, the road the bridge, everywhere was swarming with them. I said to my wife "We are surely reaching civilisation as there are plenty of cats around!" Later we stopped at the local Inn and asked about the bridge. The landlord told us that it was nicknamed the Fairy Bridge and also known as the Bridge of Cats. Not many of the locals own cats today but years ago the bridge was the haunt of a witch. What we saw has been described by many a frightened traveller. Legend says that the mystical bridge is haunted by the spirits of the witches cats!

The sample casebooks you have read suggest that it is possible for ordinary people to have glimpses of history. But far more often reported are reports I receive of people's glimpses of the future. Of course my own work, and the work of my wife Jane, often involves prophesy and seership and there a great many cases I could quote where we have predicted the future with startling accuracy. However, what I'd like to show here is that the gift of prophesy is much more widespread than you may expect. All the stories that now follow are told by ordinary people who make no claim to having special powers. The casebooks that follow are again just the tip of the iceberg of a huge mailbag that I've received on this subject. At the end of this chapter I've included a simple experiment that you can try for yourself to see if you too have the power to see the future.

'Soon after my father died I had an early morning dream about him.' says Jennifer T from Havant in Hampshire, 'He joked as he did in life, had a silver light around him and when he reached out and touched my hands he felt warm and normal. 'It's true! There is an afterlife!' I exclaimed in my dream. 'Have you met auntie Alice and grandma Coates?' I asked.

'Of course I have' relied my father 'But there's something very important that I must tell you. 'Mum is not well; she must attend to her chest.'

I had to wait until mum returned from holiday before I could tell her about the dream. 'I'm fine' she said, 'There's nothing wrong with me.' But I persisted when I noticed a nasty red lump on her chest. I insisted that she visit the doctor to get it checked.

The lump was cancerous. Mum had radiation treatment at St Mary's hospital and the cancer was caught just in time. She is now 90 years old and as fit as a fiddle.

Dreams that happen in the early morning dream phase are often the most vivid. At these times some people have 'lucid dreams' which are as clear as waking awareness. It could be argued that Jennifer's subconscious mind may have already observed her mother's red lump and told her about it in a dream. But I believe the simpler answer: Jennifer's father's spirit communicate to save her mother's life. Communication with the afterlife can sometimes be very useful and in this case helped with the future. I've discovered in the course of my work that when I make a prediction given to me by the spirit world it is invariably right. The spirit communicator tries to give helpful information that will guide their loved-one here on earth to make the best decisions.

Mediums are not in the prediction business but any information that is given them by the spirit world about the future is guided by the love of those who you know on the other side. Psychic predictions are not protected in this way and not usually as accurate as those that come via mediumship. Untrained psychic powers can cause upset and I know of many professional psychics who make very frightening predictions for people. I fail to see what spiritual purpose this sort of undisciplined work has:

'I called in on my best friend for a cup of coffee and a chat.' says Elsie from Hampshire, 'As I carried the empty cups out to the kitchen for her she said with a startled tone "I have just seen a funeral cortege follow you into the kitchen, but there's no coffin, just mourners carrying wreaths at their sides!"

'Oh Dear' I replied and left it at that.

The next day my husband, who we assumed was perfectly fit, had a massive heart attack and died. Ten years before he had made arrangements for his body to be donated to science which meant that no coffin was needed. A memorial service was held and as the premonition had predicted, there was a line of mourners carrying wreaths but no coffin.'

Unfortunately it's usually the bad things that spontaneous, uncontrolled clairvoyance reveals. Dreams are also a rich source of precognitive material but again tend be uncontrolled. Often the unconscious will tell you the gist of what's going to happen but miss out essential components. Dreams speak to us in symbols, puns, metaphors and allegories and they use these same methods when they tell us about the future as the next casebook reveals:

'I awoke from a vivid dream and told it to my husband so that I could put it into my diary later.' says a lady writing under the initials R.D., 'The dream was not pictorial; it was auditory. I had heard a name, NEVILLE, not that unusual, but I didn't know anyone by that name. I had also dreamed of the poem 'Upon Westminster Bridge' by the poet William Wordsworth.

Three months later I joined a discussion group and was introduced to a NEVILLE WESTBRIDGE. We became good friends and his ideas had a very important influence on my philosophy of life. My husband has always been very sceptical about precognition but the accuracy of this dream has made him change his tune.'

I am always pleased to hear from the older generation who often come forward with some amazing psychic stories to tell. This is mainly because they've had a lot more experience, known the tragedy of bereavement and devoted time in their later years reflecting upon the meaning of life and what follows after death. I enjoy hearing of how psychic powers played a part in their lives during WW2:

'At 9 years old I read a story book called 'Poland- Land of the Rainbow'.' says Sydney B. 'I was transfixed and my imagination roamed the country as if I was there. For years afterwards the same strange name 'Posen' kept coming to my mind. I often heard the words 'Posen, Posen, Posen' being called out to me. I heard it in my mind but it was as clear as a real voice.

'During the war I fought in Norway but was captured in 1940 and spent 5 years in various P.O.W. camps. In 1945 I was on the 1,000 mile death march from Poland through Czechoslovakia to Moosburgh Stalag 7A near Munich. During my imprisonment the Germans put us on a train to do a propaganda march around a town. The towns name was Posen.

From Posen we were taken to a near-by camp called Fort Winiary. I befriended a Polish girl in the kitchens who would give us extra food. One day she was able to get us an English book. I couldn't believe my eyes when she gave it to me: 'Poland- Land of the Rainbows' - the very book that had triggered my obsession with Posen all those years ago!!'

It makes you wonder if our future is already planned. Even as a child of 9 something told Sydney that Posen would have a monumental impact upon his life. I've always believed that we have free will and that we're given glimpses of the future so that we can avoid an adverse destiny. From an evolutionary point of view this makes sense as it would help the survival of our species. Whether there is free will or an unalterable destiny will always be a subject of debate and perhaps we'll never know the answer for certain. The next two casebook are interesting examples of this dichotomy.

Joan M from Dundee wrote to say: 'A couple of months ago, my husband woke up and told me that an old red Indian told him that ESHA NESS meant the "eye of the storm". My husband guessed that Esha Ness was a race horse so we scanned the papers for days to see if it was running. We'd almost forgotten about the dream, when we discovered Esha Ness was running in the Grand National-so naturally we backed it. We stood to win almost £5,000 but that was the year that the Grand National was abandoned because of a false starting signal. Some of the horses ran unaware of the mix up and even though Esha Ness won we lost out.

'My husband firmly believes that because he backed the horse, things happened the way they did. Can a person control fate in this way or is this just a bizarre coincidence?'

Many psychic people have spirit guides from the North American Indian tradition and I wonder if Joan's husband's guide was proving his reality by giving him the winner of the Grand National! I've certainly found that my own spirit guides can play tricks in this way. For example I can sometimes stand in front of an audience and tell a string of people what six numbers they choose every week for the lottery. The odds for doing this are of course billions to one but can I predict the numbers for next week? No, not a single one. I can be very infuriating but I think that this says something about the nature of spiritual gifts: They cannot be used solely for material gain.

Perhaps what's meant to be will be as the next casebook, sent to me by Miss Dolores G Edinburgh, may prove:

'I dreamed of looking at a pools coupon and saying to my daughter "Oohh look at the strange way the draws have come up. They're all at the bottom of the form!". I told my daughter about the dream but nonetheless did my usual numbers that week. Then, yes you guessed it, the result was that there were 11 draws in the last 12 entries. I was upset of course but not for long. Two weeks later my regular numbers came up and I won £1,510! I believe that despite not following my dream I was meant to win.'

Maybe, if Dolores G had paid attention to her dream she may have won the pools twice! We'll never unravel all the mysteries of destiny but I'm sure she deserves her good-fortune.

Of course prediction is one of the areas of Jane and my work that the newspapers are eager to tap although as I try to explain it is not the most important part of our work. When Princess Diana met Dodie the *Sunday Mirror* asked me to make some predictions about what would happen. I told the journalist various things that came yo me and said 'But none of this may happen because Prince Charles is going to be involved in a serious car accident that will change the course of events.'

The journalist said that she couldn't print this and I got it wrong. But a car accident did of course change the course of events but I'd seen the wrong person involved. Prediction and all the psychic gifts are so easily miss-seen or misheard. Here's an excellent example sent to me that shows just how subtle clairvoyance can be:

'I often have premonitions about events that I read about later in the paper.' says Mr DP from Hampshire, 'The most disturbing experience happened recently and while I was wide awake. All day long I kept hearing in my head 'The Queen is dead. Long live the King!' It ran over and over in my thoughts like a catchy song that you can't get out of your mind. I was beginning to wonder if the Queen was going to die.

'The next day it was announced that Diana had died in a car crash. Across Buckingham Palace was soon draped a banner saying 'Diana- Queen of Hearts'. The Queen had died- but not the one I expected.'

Now try out another test and see if you too can see into the distant reaches of time :

Can you 'see' the future?

There's a state between sleeping and waking that psychologists call hypnagogic dreaming. These 'dreams' are a flow of vivid but brief mental images and can occur just before you fall off to sleep. The images can sometimes possess an overwhelming sense of reality, with much detail and supersaturated colour. Some psychologists have pointed out a similarity between the images seen in a crystal ball and the experience of hypnagogic imagery. And, like the crystal ball hypnagogic dreams contain potent omens and visions of the future.

Harness their power and you can use your dreams to see the future. You can become the psychic newscaster.

Here's a dream experiment to try:

1. First you must choose a target subject to dream about. Select something that you're interested in but not emotionally involved with so that your inner hopes and fears don't influence your insights. For this experiment we'll try to dream about next week's main news stories.

2. Put a copy of a newspaper by the side of your bed before retiring. Touch it so that you focus your attention as you prepare to go to sleep. Now ask yourself "What important news headlines will be in this paper over the coming week?"

3. As you drop off to sleep you will try to stimulate hypnagogic mental imagery and manipulate the visions. To stimulate this awareness it is important to completely relax but don't let yourself fall to sleep straight away. The knack of hypnagogic dreaming is to hold your awareness between waking and the onset of sleep.

4. As you teeter on the brink of sleep watch your thoughts but don't follow them. Be the observer of yourself. Instead of thinking in words, try to think in pictures. For example, you think "I ought to do the gardening tomorrow." Convert this into a picture- see the garden, the flowers, the sky. Gradually you'll stimulate a flow of visual imagery. Many scenes and pictures will flash before your mind's eye.

5. Now imagine a blank copy of the newspaper is in front of you. Next transfer the stream of imagery onto the white pages. By linking the images you are encouraging your subconscious mind to associate the images it throws up with the future headlines. You trigger your precognition.

6. Then imagine the images changing to printed words. Try to read them. At first you may just pick up one or two words. You may only see "Politician" but the next day you read "Politician in sex scandal with vicar" Now pull yourself back from your reverie and frantically write down your predictions before they fade. .

7. If you see nothing let go, drop off to sleep and instead write your dream down in the morning. By programming yourself to dream of future events you most probably will. You may find an accurate prediction are contained in next morning's dream as symbolic allegories of future events.

4 HORRIFIC PREDICTION BY EDGAR ALLAN POE

Dinner on 25 July 1884 will always be remembered in our family because of the unusual main course, my great grandfather's cousin, a 17 year-old cabin boy called Richard Parker.

Our family roots are in Woolston on Southampton water. And, like many of my family before and after him, Richard ran away to sea. He boarded the *Mignonette*, a ship built on the Thames for an Australian millionaire who wanted to explore the Great Barrier Reef.

The captain of the vessel, Tom Dudley had trouble commissioning a crew for her long maiden voyage, so to avoid delay her owner went on ahead by ocean liner. Later the *Mignonette*, with Edwin Stephens as mate and Edmund Brooks as hand, left Southampton, their last port-of-call, for the long haul to Australia.

It was Richard Parker's first voyage on the high seas. Thomas Dudley was a sturdy and resourceful captain, Stephens and Brooks went about their duties efficiently, but Richard had problems. Captain Dudley wrote in his log: "June 28th. Break in the weather. First heavy seas. Yawl sound and handles well. Cabin boy a poor sailor."

They were 1,600 miles from land when the South Atlantic hurricane broke. *The Mignonette* was hit by huge waves and sank in five minutes: "July 5th. Hit by hurricane on port beam. Mast away, sails torn. Enormous seas. Mignonette sinks. Take to open dinghy. Very little food."

In the panic to board the lifeboats, Parker threw their water barrel and provisions into the sea expecting them to float- they sank. Dudley bravely climbed aboard the wreck to see what else could be salvaged, but all he managed to grab were two tins of turnips which he mistook for meat.

The turnips did not last long between four people and survival was looking less and less likely. They caught a splash of rainwater in a cape and Dudley, using a clasp knife tied to an oar, was able to kill a turtle. The knife was to come in useful again later.

They were drifting from the shipping lanes, pushed onward by violent storms. Parker began to drink sea water: "July 16th. No sight of shipping. Estimate at least seven more days with contrary winds. Parker sick. Sea water. Turtle hard to digest. Raw and oily."

Parker was becoming weak and delirious with thirst and much of the time was in a semi-conscious state. The others were exhausted, weary and desperate, but determined to survive as long as possible. But the ordeal was becoming too much for the cabin boy: his pale gaunt body shook with the effects of dehydration, his mind raced with thoughts of home and hatred for his first sea voyage. Dudley did his best to keep up morale: "July 23rd. Parker delirious. Must have drunk more sea water. Crew in poor spirits- nerves frayed. Need food desperately."

Stories about cannibalism at sea were familiar to these men. Some seamen argued that it was defensible in extreme conditions; and there were many songs, sea shanties and poems which developed the theme. Captain Dudley considered drawing lots to decide which of them should die to save the others, but then Parker took a turn for the worse. They had been adrift now for 16 days with no sign of land.

"July 24th. Have finally reached a decision. The three of us have decided that the boy must die."

Captain Dudley persuaded Stephens and Brooks that the boy lying desperately ill at the bottom of the boat should be sacrificed for the survival of them all. It must have been an agonising debate, particularly for Dudley, who was known as a man of exemplary character.

Brooks was the hardest to convince and balked when it came to the moment for action. He went as far away as possible while Dudley and Stephens said some prayers over Parker's sleeping body. Then, Dudley shook the lad by the shoulder and said: "Wake up Dick, my boy, your time has come." Stephens held the boy's legs.

"What me sir? No don't..... " they cut his throat and caught the streaming blood in a rusty bailer. The two men, dying of dehydration and half mad with fear and doubt, drank the warm blood. Captain Dudley with his clasp knife dissected the bleeding corpse. Even Brooks, his body tormented with thirst and hunger, joined in the grisly meal. (It is said that human flesh tastes like sweet pork.)

"I offered up a prayer most fervently that God might forgive us for such an act," Dudley said weeping at his trial. "It was my decision to take the boy's life, but it was justified by an over-riding necessity. As a result I have lost only one member of my crew in circumstances in which all would otherwise have perished."

The meal kept them alive until 29 July when they were sighted by the *S S Montezuma*. An aptly named vessel, as Montezuma was the Aztec king who, to the horror of the bloodthirsty Spanish conquistador Cortes, ate the flesh of sacrificed children. Captain Dudley and his remaining crew made no attempt to hide the dismembered corpse of the sacrificed teenager as the ship approached. The *Montezuma's* German captain had Richard Parker's remains buried at sea. Dudley Stephens and Brooks made no attempt to hide the shame of their desperate act of survival. Soon after the ship docked in the Cornish port of Falmouth, they were arrested and stood trial at Exeter Assizes, in Devon, with Brooks as the chief prosecution witness. All three men broke down and cried under cross-examination.

The Victorian public were shocked by the ghastly events reported in *The Times*, but were surprisingly sympathetic. Generally, the three accused were cheered on. Judge Baron Huddleston was impressed by Dudley's character and sterling courage.

The legal position was contradictory: on the one hand the men had committed an act of murder; yet if a situation arises where a man is faced with the necessity to kill in order to survive, the law states that he is innocent of murder so long as he has the victim's consent. Many other legal points also challenged the men's guilt but one of the conclusions was that the killing was premeditated and therefore unjustified in English law. The jury's conclusion was unprecedented as they expressed their ignorance of whether the men were guilty of murder. In the end it was decided that they were and the death sentence was passed with a recommendation to mercy.

There was an immediate appeal and a re-trial using a classic defence, duress of circumstances, which is still quoted in courts today. The seamen were found guilty of manslaughter did six months' hard labour and disappeared from view.

The story has a strange twist in its tail. Half a century before the grisly events, in 1837, Edgar Allan Poe wrote *The Narrative of Arthur Gordon Pym of Nantucket*. This short story tells of four shipwrecked men who, after many days' privation, drew lots to decide who should be killed and eaten. The cabin boy drew the short straw. His name was Richard Parker!

"He made no resistance whatever and fell instantly dead when stabbed in the back by Peters [....] Having in some measure appeased the raging thirst which consumed us by drinking the blood of the victim, and having by common consent taken off the hands, feet and head, and throwing them, together with the entrails, into the sea, we devoured the rest of the body, piecemeal....."

My cousin Nigel Parker was the first to notice the link between the Poe story and actual events and wrote about it in a letter to The Sunday Times of 5 May 1974. The author of a book about strange coincidences told me that sometime after The Sunday Times letter had been published, he casually mentioned it to John Beloff at the University of Edinburgh, who had, that day, written about it in his journal.

Nigel's father, Keith, thought that Richard's story would make an interesting theme for a radio play and began to plan a synopsis. At that time, to supplement his writer's income, he reviewed books for Macmillan publishers. The first book to arrive through the post was *The Sinking of the Mignonette*. A few weeks later he was asked to review another play, among a collection of short plays, called *The Raft*. It was a comedy for children with nothing sinister about it at all, apart from the cover illustration. Three men seemed to threaten a young boy, which is completely out of keeping with the play's tone. *The Raft* was written by someone called Richard Parker.

In the summer of 1993, my parents took in three Spanish language students. My father told them about Richard Parker one evening over supper. (probably in an attempt to keep the food bills down)

The television was on in the background. All conversation stopped when a local programme started talking about the remarkable story. Dad went on to break the silence by saying how weird coincidences always occur whenever Richard's tale is mentioned. He told them about Edgar Allan Poe.

All three girls went white. "Look what I bought today," said one. She reached into her bag and pulled out a copy of the Poe story. "So have I!"

said the other two girls in unison. They had all gone shopping independently that day, yet all three girls had bought the very same book containing the *The Narrative of Arthur Gordon Pym of Nantucket* which had foreseen the Richard Parker story.

Although Parker's body was buried at sea, a headstone was erected in his memory at Pear Tree Churchyard near his birthplace in Woolston, Southampton.

Sacred to the memory of Richard Parker, aged 17, who died at sea, July 25 th 1884, after nineteen days dreadful suffering in an open boat in the tropics, having been wrecked in the yacht Mignonette
"Though He slay me yet will I trust in Him" *Job XIII: 15*
"Lord, lay not this sin to their charge" *Acts VII: 60*

The memorial only hints at the tragic story that surrounds his death.

It was rumoured that the experience caused Stephens to go mad and that Brooks too suffered and spent his life in mental turmoil. Captain Dudley fled to Australia to start a new life as a ship's chandler. He is said to have also secretly sent money to support Parker's sister through school, before dying of bubonic plague.

My grandfather told of a local family who were paid by the captain to keep the stone clean in perpetuity. they were so ashamed of accepting his money that they asked for their name to be kept secret and they would only clean the stone in the dead of night. In the 1930's it was easily found by being the brightest stone in the churchyard. In recent decades the gravestone was neglected, but was restored recently with a grant of £350 from Southampton City Council.

I published the above story in a magazine called *The Fortean Times* and it was later covered by the *Sunday Telegraph*. Understanding how strange 'Richard Parker Coincidences' often happen to anyone who read about the story I invited readers to write to me if anything weird happened to them. It wasn't long before the coincidences started to happen. The first happened on the day I bought *The Fortean Times* to read my article. I had it with me when I went round to my brother Ian's house. There I met my cousin Angela and her then boyfriend who was studying to be a lawyer. 'As a would be lawyer you'll be interested by my latest article.' I said passing the magazine to him. He'd never been told the Richard Parker story but he had only just read about it a few moments ago. He took me over to my brother's dining room table where he'd been doing his studies. There on the table was the book

Cannibalism and the Common Man open on the page concerning the case he'd been reading about Judge Baron Huddleston's decision concerning the cannibalism of Richard Parker by Dudley and Stephens.

Now I wouldn't blame you if you thought I was making all this up but I'm afraid the coincidences get even worse. Here's a few of the weird things that happened to my readers:

Janice Robertson from Loanhead in Midlothian wrote to say: 'My husband and I were on holiday in Guernsey staying in the Duke of Normandie Hotel in St Peter Port. As I read your article I was sat at a table in the bar and on this table is carved the story of the shipwreck and fate of the same cabin boy. I was quite sceptical about this story and could hardly believe it when I saw it in both places.' Another person Joyce Robinson from Minehead had a similar experience saying that she read the story in the *Sunday Telegraph* then again later that same morning in a book called *The Blue Bays of Cornwall*. Also Jo Chipperfield from Hull read the story in newspaper and then moments later by pure chance read about the story again in an obscure book called *Fishy Yarns*.

Some readers also rang me to tell about their weird experiences connected with reading this story. James Plaskett from Hastings rang to tell me about how a family in Hascombe Godalming had bought the oak door of the prison cell that had closed on Dudley and Stephens and how there were two other Richard Parker's who had brought bad luck at sea. One was hung as the leader of the Nore mutiny in 1797 and another died when the Francis Speight floundered in 1846. On board a number of seamen had been eaten. He'd experience a similar coincidence to the other writers reading about the story twice in the same day. "I expect something stranger will happen soon" I said. And it did within seconds. We soon realised that we were both sat in front of our computer screens, which is not unusual, but were both playing computer chess. I very rarely do this during the day but I needed a break from writing. James Plaskett is a chess grand master.

The strangest coincidence was sent to me by Carlton Morgan from Newport who wrote to say 'After reading the article I received a telephone call from a friend, asking me to help him compose a letter to his employer, Mr Dudley, with whom he was in a legal dispute. We took the letter to a local advice centre to check our legal position.

'During the course of the interview my pal was told that Dudley was disregarding acceptable legal procedures. Then we went for coffee, and a discussion over the mindset of the boss class ensued, 'Well, I reckon this riding roughshod over legal procedures is in his blood' said my friend. 'This guy is into tracing his ancestors, and one of them was a sea captain who was done for eating cabin boy Richard Parker without drawing lots....'"

A brave attempt to link coincidence, ESP, and frontier physics was made by the psychical researcher Arthur Koestler. He suggested that there was is a fundamental law that governs all these three which, as yet, we do not know. Even the great mind of Koestler was perplexed and he admits in his book *The Roots of Coincidence* that his theories are only a first step in a darkened room.

It will probably be a physicist or cosmologist that will come up with a plausible theory that explains coincidence. In the strange world of fundamental particles scientists have found that in certain cases the laws of causality (the law that cause precedes effect) seems to not apply. For example some sub atomic particles like quarks and leptons can exist in more than one place at the same time.

Physicists talk about the 'uncertainty principle' which in simple terms means that, according to Quantum theory, an electron or any other particle in its natural state has no specific identity or agenda. It has only a potential existence as an aspect of what is called a wave function. When something intrudes on this condition, such as the physicist's experiment, the wave collapses and the electron appears as one of its possible states of size, energy or time. In other words, the material world is not as concrete as we think. It's full of paradoxes, the most intriguing of which is time.

Time went off the rails for *Silence of the Lambs* actor Anthony Hopkins when he visited Vienna in 1973 to discuss his new film *The Girl from Petrovka* with the book's author George Feifer. Unfortunately, explained Feifer, his original copy with his important margin notes had been stolen from his car two years earlier in London. The important creative notes, that would be useful for the film, would have to be done again.

Coincidence came to their rescue. Soon after signing the contract for his film role, explained Hopkins to the weary Feifer, he had scoured London for a copy of 'Girl from Petrovka'. No shops stocked it so he headed home. Hopkins noticed an open parcel by his seat in London's Leicester Square underground station. It was a copy of the novel he was looking for.

Hopkins handed it to Feifer - it was Feifer's original copy, complete with the margin notes, stolen some two years earlier!

Did Anthony Hopkins' desire to find a copy of *Girl from Petrovka* somehow influenced events to attract the book to him? It may be that meaningful coincidences happen because of the influence our unconscious mind has upon the environment. Or perhaps the world that we see outside of ourselves and the world within our head are one and the same? The psychoanalyst Carl Jung proposed that psychological events corresponded with and perhaps influence physical events- what he called the "unexpected parallelism between psychic and physical events". He called his theory synchronicity.

By synchronicity Jung meant meaningful coincidence: two events which take place at the same time, and are relevant to one another, but which take place independently. (a literal definition of the word means "at the same time") Time, argued Jung, was more like a web than a straight line of cause and effect. He said: "Anything done at a particular moment of time has the qualities of that moment in time"

This is why fortune-telling works. When a psychic casts the tarot cards, rune stones or throws dice the coincidental fall of cards etc. are interpreted as an accurate indication of the true nature of a situation. Jung himself was particularly interested in the Chinese oracle book called the 'I Ching' which is normally cast by throwing three coins. Together with a natal chart of a horoscope he would use these oracles to diagnose his patients psychiatric problems.

Jung experienced many meaningful coincidences himself. On one occasion he was helping a patient understand the symbolism of the Egyptian scarab beetle that had featured in the patient's dream. As he did this a large brightly coloured beetle, similar in appearance to a scarab, flew into the room.

5 AMAZING SPIRIT MESSAGES

Many sceptics argue that mediums and psychics gather their information by fishing for information or by watching the facial expressions and body language of their sitters. I hope that the following stories you will now read go some way to disprove this. In each case Jane and I have never met any of the people involved prior to their consultation and, as you will see, there is no way we could have cheated by looking up the information in the public record office. Versions of some of the stories that follow have appeared in various magazines and were authenticated by independent journalists.

It was years since 25 year old Ken Reynolds had ridden a motorcycle and hardly ever as a pinion passenger. But that was the last journey Ken was ever to make. Moments after leaving home the motorbike was involved in a head on collision and Ken and his friend were killed.

"I can't find words to adequately describe what I felt" says his mother Pat Reynolds from Bitterne in Southampton. "One moment Ken was here and in the next he was gone. I felt empty. Worse than empty. It was like having a big dark hole inside of you- but it had jagged edges."

Pat sunk into a dark depression after the loss of her son. She shut herself away from the world and felt that life wasn't worth living. From the day after he died Ken seemed to make his presence known to her. ""Strange things started to happen around the house." continues Pat, "The lights would start going on and off, Ken's photo kept falling of the mantelpiece and I saw the morning's dishes lift and move by themselves across the kitchen table. I began to feel that Ken was trying to get in touch with me."

Pat began a quest to find out if Ken had survived physical death. "I gained a lot of comfort from visiting my local Spiritualist Church" says Pat "I had a number of messages and went to see a medium privately. The medium, Matthew Smith, was even able to tell me his name straight away and told me other details known only to myself."

Pat was beginning to feel comforted but that gaping hole inside her still wouldn't go away. "I needed something more. I had to find away to get in touch with Ken directly."

It was then that Pat met me at a Psychic Fair in Southampton. "I sat down for a tarot reading with Craig" says Pat "But he pushed the cards aside and said that it was more important that he communicates with my son who he said I'd only recently lost."

"Craig described Ken's personality perfectly and told me how he died and gave me many factual things about him. In particular, I remember Craig saying that the song 'Lemon tree oh so pretty' was significant. We had a lemon tree in the garden when we lived in South Africa."

A little later Pat booked a private consultation with me at her home and away from the clatter of the fair that we both found distracting. "Craig gave me marvellous proof that Ken was all right in his new life" says Pat, "Ken told Craig how his friend Claire had her hair cropped and had now got a new job in Bristol. He extended his love to his friends Jonathan and Colleen. He also told how he had met his uncles George and grandfather Percy and how he loved his gardening. Craig said how I'd been told to buy a ruby ring in Ken's memory but said my son was joking that I hadn't paid enough for it! And he even gave Ken's birthday date and said that a new baby would be born on the same date. It happened as he said

"But, apart from the hard facts, it was Craig's description of Ken's personality that was most convincing. He joked and laughed with Ken and exhibited the same dry humour and tongue in cheek tone. I remember Craig saying that Ken said 'I died with my boots on' When Ken died he was wearing the new boots that he'd only just bought."

But Pat's search was still not over. I invited Pat to join his circle that meets once a week with the objective of communicating with the spirit world and developing the clairvoyant abilities of those who want to progress. Ken was now able to communicate regularly with his mother and could even speak directly to Pat when I was in a deep trance state.

Pat's own psychic abilities have now started to flower. "I still get depressed about Ken when I think of the wasted years and the grandchildren from him that I will never have. I miss his touch and his humour. But at least I know that he's happy where he is. And best of all I can talk to him whenever I want to"

Pat's own mediumship is developing at a remarkable rate. I'm so pleased for her. I know that mediumship has helped her and know that she in turn will help many other people in their grief.

The next story you will read, this time from Jane's casebook, is similar to the Pat's story in many ways but it's very interesting to compare the stories and see how another brave woman copes with her worst nightmare come true. Diana Ashton from Southampton couldn't come to terms with her son's death -until she spoke to him through Jane....

Diana's son Mark just loved motorbikes. He also loved life, family, people and owned a pet chinchilla dog and two other dogs. But he really loved motorbikes and would spend hours tinkering and fine tuning his pride and joy.

"I'll never forget that night in August 1994" continues Diana "Mark had been helping me decorate before going out to play pool. It was an exciting time as the next day Mark was to sign the agreement for the mortgage on a flat he was to purchase and share with his friend David. Every mother is a little sad to when their children finally leave home. He'd be in his flat by the weekend."

"As he left, he smiled and said: "Bye, Mum." Then he came back into the lounge, kissed me and said: 'I won't say good-bye, I'll see you later.'"

Later that evening the police came to the door bearing terrible news. Twenty four year old Mark had been in collision with a car. The accident had killed him instantly. "'Not our wonderful Mark,' I sobbed uncontrollably, as my husband Peter tried to console me.

"I thought the grief would tear me apart but I kept going in those first few days by organising the funeral. I dressed him myself, putting on his favourite jeans, shirt and blazer. At his side, I put notes that friends and family had written to him, saying their good-byes. Finally when it was time to leave, I placed a single red rose in his hands, kissed him tenderly and whispered: 'Goodnight, my darling.'

"They say time is a great healer, but as the months passed I couldn't get the image of Mark in his coffin out of my mind.

"Whenever I talked of Mark's accident and told people that he was on a motorcycle at the time, they seem to think that it was his fault almost in the belief that all motorcyclists are 'accidents waiting to happen'. And matters were made worse because of the post-mortem and by not knowing when the inquest was to be held and worrying about its outcome. My GP prescribed me some anti depressive tablets and I received some professional counselling but that terrible aching pain just wouldn't go away. One of my biggest fears was that Mark's spirit was trapped in some limbo state and that he was unhappy.

"I'd spend hours in his room. 'I'm keeping it exactly as he left it,' I sobbed to Peter.

"Wracked with grief, I'd gaze at his pictures on the wall. Some showed him in his biking leathers and crash helmet at Goodwood racetrack in Sussex, where he loved to compete.

"He'd always made such a success of everything. As well as his job as a salesman, he loved go-karting and his trophies took pride of place on his shelves.

"As I looked at them, my gaze would always wander to that special container alongside them- the one holding Mark's ashes. We'd never discussed death with him, so we had no idea where he'd want his final resting place to be.

"Everything else in my life had lost meaning. My marriage had begun to suffer and I'd contemplated suicide. Then, in May 1996, a concerned friend suggested I should visit a clairvoyant she'd been recommended. 'She's supposed to be excellent' she said"

Diana telephoned Jane.

"My fingers trembled as I picked up the receiver. But before I could utter a word, a woman's voice said: "You're ringing about your son Mark. He wants to talk to you.'

"My head began to spin. How did she know his name? I was stunned.

"' He's standing beside me holding a red rose in his hand' continued Jane "the one you put in the coffin. When you come to see me, I'll tell you what he wants to say.'

"So, on 19 April 1996, 20 months after Mark's accident, I found myself going to see a perfect stranger about my son.

"Jane started talking about mark the moment I sat down in her living-room. 'He's here in the room with us now, Diana,' she said. 'He's tall and good-looking. He's wearing jeans, a shirt and a blazer. He says the notes you put next to him in his coffin are still in his pocket.'

A strange feeling swept over me. I must have looked dazed. She couldn't possibly have known the things she told me. I looked around expecting to see Mark

"Jane smiled. 'Only I can see him,' she explained gently. I imagined him standing close, his big beautiful brown eyes sparkling.

"Jane also gave me other amazing facts about Mark that completely convinced me that he was not only with us but happy. He said how the accident was not his fault, how I still kept his Arai racing helmet and he talked of my feelings when I first saw his body. He joked about how after his death I'd had a photo of him enlarged 'The bigger the better, I deserve it' were his words. He spoke of how his friend Lee was still visiting car boot sales and extended his thoughts for his motorcycle friends, especially David. He even said how I'd tried on his clothes- a fact that not even my husband knew- and how I had recently bought a large toy dog and laid it across his bed!

"With tears streaming down my face I listened as she continued: 'Mark's worried about you. He says he wants you to get over his death. He's happy now and wants you to get on with your life. He says you should stop keeping his room as a shrine and that you must not hang on to his things any longer. He wants you to give them away. He's saying it's time to let go. One other thing' Jane went on. 'Mark says it's time to get rid of his ashes. He'd liked them to be scattered at Goodwood.'

"I sat stunned. There was no doubt in my mind that the words were coming from Mark. 'But how can this be?' I stammered.

" 'He says to tell you it's like in the film *Ghost*,' she replied. 'He can see and hear everything that's going on.'

"Then she added: 'He's being called back to the spirit world now, Diana. He says he won't say good-bye, just that he'll see you later.'

"When I returned home, I listened to the tape I'd made of Jane speaking. For the first time since Mark's death I felt a spark of hope.

"The following week, we went to Goodwood, as Mark had requested. 'Take care, my love,' I whispered as I sprinkled his ashes next to the starting line on the evening of Thursday 2nd May 1996.

"Although it was difficult letting him go, as we drove back to our home in Southampton I felt as if a huge weight had lifted. 'This is a new beginning,' I thought to myself. 'It's what Mark wants.'

"Over the following months, I began to sort through his belongings. It was difficult to part with them as I felt they were my last link with my son.

"But I've done it- the only thing I've kept is a tiny model of a motorbike Mark made just before he died. I am now no longer have to take medication for my depression and don't have to visit a counsellor. I know that without the help I have received from Mark and the Spirit World through Jane I certainly would have never recovered. Even worse I would probably have committed the ultimate sin and taken my own life!

"I owe Jane so much because she changed my life. I am now at peace with myself. I still see her sometimes and she always lets me know how Mark's getting on.

"I still go to his room whenever I want to be with him. Knowing Mark's still with me is such a great comfort and, one day, I truly believe we'll meet up again."

Many of the things Jane and I have told to our sitters have not been known to them at the time of their consultation but have later been proved correct when they've checked the information with family and friends afterwards. This is important because it goes to prove that what we do is not mind reading. The next story is also about the special bond between mother and son but this time it's the mother who talks to her son from beyond:

Abandoned in a Moses basket on the steps of Dr Barnardo's home in Stepney London, Dudley Godfrey spent a lifetime wondering what his mother was like and why she would abandon him as a new born babe. "For years it was impossible to know the truth" he says "I was not eligible for a birth certificate and Barnardo's refused to give me any information about my background. All I had was my fantasy. Perhaps my mother was unfit, a prostitute, or she just didn't want to know me? It's hard for anyone from a secure family to understand the inner anguish caused from not knowing who you are or what your roots are."

In 1995 at the age of 53 a charity worker called at Dudley's property business in Burseldon Southampton. She was collecting for Dr Barnardo's. The lady informed him that it was nowadays easy for ex-Barnardo's children to get their Birth Certificate. She told him how to do it.

As the high powered General Manager of a successful company Dudley wasted no time in putting plans into action. "I went straight down to the registrar and got the certificate." continues Dudley "To my surprise I was born miles away. Next I instructed my secretary to find out the name of the town's local parson and see if he knew anything about my family. Fortunately he was a keen genealogist and offered to check the parish records and would write me a full family tree."

"When his report landed on my desk I dashed to the car and drove to London? to see my last remaining relative- my mother's sister. Within an hour and a half I was at her doorstep, my heart pounding hard."

Dudley Godfrey discovered that his now dead father was the husband of his long lost aunt. Clearly a terrible family problem had occurred at Dudley's birth that had resulted in his abandonment. But at last now Dudley knew who he was and a little about his background. "The most startling thing was meeting my half-brother. He was my clone. Not only did he look like me but had the same body language and even talked like me.
"Sadly I also discovered that my mother had died a long time ago and I resolved my self to the fact there was no way I would ever talk to her or know her." Soon afterwards Dudley read about the medium Craig Hamilton-Parker who worked in the nearby town of Eastleigh. The article described how Craig could talk with people who have gone over into the Spirit World. Dudley telephoned me and arranged an appointment.

"Immediately I walked into his consultation room Craig asked me if I knew of an Uncle George who he said had been talking to him during his meditations. George, who I had called Uncle, had brought me up from the age of two after leaving Barnardo's. 'He died of TB' said Craig 'And says that his wife's name was Lotty. Also, he would have been very sceptical about mediums as he'd had a very strict religious upbringing. He loved the countryside and was a farm labourer.'

"I couldn't believe what I was hearing. Craig was reeling off the facts. Facts that he could never have checked through public records. By now tears were rolling down my cheeks.

"Craig continued by saying 'There's something about him that only you and he ever knew about. George tells me that he was a secret drinker.' That clinched it. I was the only person in the world that knew this. It was a standing joke between us."

"Craig went on to tell me about how I'd been in Doctor Barnardo's, he told me about my deceased wife Betty and that she was aware that I'd been having problems with my kidneys and how she wanted to pass on her love to my daughter and two sons. She was pleased, Craig said, that despite everything I was making a success of my life and was reasonably happy."

Then perhaps the most important person of all came through. "I've got to give you a message from a lady with the name Grace" I said, "She died of womb cancer at the age of thirty and she's so sorry for everything that happened when you we little."

At last Dudley's mother had made contact. "Your mum is telling me that she didn't want to give you to Dr Barnardo's. It broke her heart but there was nothing that she could do. She was forced to do what she did, there was no way she could keep me, and she regretted it for the rest of her short life. She loves you, her only child, very much."

"Craig told me that I must ask my Aunt about this and various other events that transpired at the time of my birth. Immediately afterwards I telephoned my Aunt and asked her about all the things that were said during the consultation. She was dumfounded. 'How on earth do you know these things!' she exclaimed. But that was mum's and my little secret.

"I am not in the habit of visiting psychics or mediums" says Dudley, "For me it was my first and perhaps only exposure to these things. But it helped me a great deal and unloaded a tremendous weight from my shoulders. At last I believe that I have been able to talk to the mother that I never knew. I now have a photograph of mum but the greatest comfort of all is knowing that her spirit's close to me and that one day we will meet and talk about everything that happened. My lifelong fear that I would never be able to talk to her just isn't true.""

Although mediumship is primarily about proving that we survive death and bringing comfort and solace to the bereaved there are times when the spirit world make contact in order to give a warning about the future. Unfortunately most people are have no idea of how superior mediumship is to fortune telling. Some insist I read the tarot cards as they want 'nothing to do with spooks and all that'.

I've spoken to my Tibetan spirit guide about this.

The Spiritualist part of me believes in free will and that we should take 'personal responsibility' for our destiny. The Tibetan Buddhist influences around me tell of the principles of karma and acceptance. In addition I believe in reincarnation and that I am influenced by two of my past lives as a somewhat rebellious Tibetan monk. (I believe one of these lives may have been around about 1230 when Genghis Khan and the Mongols dominated the world scene and another at about 1650 as a painter of mandalas during the time of the fifth Dali Lama.)

My main concerns about fortune telling are that people will become either spiritually paralysed if they are told something bad about the future or complacent if they are shown something good. Most people see a fortune teller because they are unable to cope with their worry. They just want someone to tell them 'everything will be all right'

In answer to my questions my Tibetan spirit guide told me that the objective of divination is to assess the person's situation and recommend ways to respond to it and take remedial action. Although there is no escaping their karma they can trigger the latent positive potential in themselves and others. In this way the individual is not stepping outside of the laws of cause and effect but instead using merit to awaken the forces of good karma.

When Joan B came to see me the spirit world were quick to give her advice about the future:

"If you don't act immediately I see you losing everything." I said my sitter

Joan B from Bournemouth. Apparently she had booked the consultation with me to see if I could give her any insight into the sorry state of her marriage.

"Craig communicated with many people I'd known who had passed into the spirit." says Joan "In particular he spoke to my Nan who told him that her wedding ring had recently broke in two. This had happened recently and Craig said it was also a symbol of what was happening in my own life.

"'Your husband owns a restaurant' said Craig. 'You must be very, very careful as he's trying to sell it without you finding out.

"Craig was right, we did own a restaurant but it would be impossible for him to sell it. It had only been open for two years and who'd buy a restaurant that had traded for such a short time?

"Craig insisted that I make enquiries. If I don't act, he said, the money will disappear to America and you'll be left with nothing. He said that a female solicitor would help me get a court order to prohibit the sale. The judge would look favourably upon my case."

It was Joan's 'dead' grandparents who were telling me all this information. Her grandmother told Joan many facts about herself but one fact in particular proved it was her. "Craig said that my Grandmother had two wedding rings and that I now had one and my sister the other which was right. He also identified the problems that I was having with my daughter and how to deal with them" says Joan.

Immediately after the consultation Joan employed a female solicitor and asked her to make enquiries about the restaurant. She discovered that it was for sale and a buyer had been found. Joan also heard rumours that her ex-husband was planning to move to America. "We went to court immediately we knew the facts and took out an injunction to stop the sale" continues Joan "The result was that me and my two children we given a fair settlement and received a substantial sum of money. If I hadn't listened to the clairvoyant we would now be destitute. I've still got a lot of emotional problems to resolve but at least now our financial future is secure."

People come to see Jane and myself for all sorts of reasons. For example Tracey Roberts from London came to see me advice about a neighbour who was causing trouble. She found out much more than she bargained for.

"You're either a hairdresser or something to do with TV was the first thing Craig said when I sat down for the psychic consultation. He could never have guessed that I'd just embarked on a career as an actress. 'Although you've come along today to sort out a material problem there's something more important you should know about. Although you are black your step father Jim was white. He wants you to know that you've a four year old sister that you've never met and who one day will want to get in touch with you.'

"I had a sneaking feeling that what Craig was saying was true but had never really wanted to face up to it. There were family rumours, but I'd always thought that they were just that- rumours.'

Tracey was also given the information she needed about her neighbour dispute. I told her how it was a Chinese lady with a disabled child who was causing the problem but there was some good news from the spirit world- the lady would be moving soon and everybody, including the Chinese lady and her son, would be happy. I also told Tracy about her friend Ronnie who died of bowel cancer. "I had no idea how she had died but found out later it was bowl cancer - just as Craig had said." says Tracey.

"When I got home I decided to check out what Craig had said about my lost half sister. I hadn't seen my father since I was ten years old and it wasn't the sort of question I wanted to ask Mum. My only option was to ask my sister in Jamaica. At first she wasn't forthcoming when I rang her but when she discovered how much I already knew the true facts came out. Yes we did have a half sister- and she's just had her fourth birthday."

If you've been read any of my newspaper columns that answers letters from readers who've had a psychic experience you won't be surprised to know that most people, at sometime in their life, have had a psychic experience. In fact the letters I've published in my columns represent only a fraction of thousands sent to me. It appears that many people- perhaps everyone- has the potential to be psychic.

But not everyone should be a professional. There are many charlatan clairvoyants around who do more harm than good. To know what your clients are going through you have to have suffered yourself. You need to know what it is to have the most important things in your life taken away from you. But sometimes the news from the other is good news indeed.

Unlike many of the people we've covered in this series Bob Morris from Gosport in Hampshire is no stranger to psychic phenomena. He is himself a Spiritualist healer and regularly visits mediums to keep in touch with those he knows in the afterlife. "I can't understand why so many people are antagonistic to the claims of mediums and healers" says Bob, "I have been involved in the subject for a great many years and have been guided and helped by the spirit people throughout my life. I believe that mediumship can really help people overcome grief and offers a wonderful philosophy for life."

When Bob came for a consultation with the me it was M. who communicated with him from the afterlife. As the sitting progressed I said "You're a very lucky man. Fortune has smiled upon you just recently. you've had a windfall and you should expect another soon."

Unbeknown to me Bob had, only a few weeks before, won a Jackpot £50,000 on a scratch card for the national lottery. "Strangely enough I woke up that morning and just knew that I was going to win. I remembered the time from long ago when I had the same feeling. On that occasion we were very hard up and the last thing the family could afford was a Sunday joint- it cost over two shillings! I announced that I'd win on the Tuesday and said so every day. Nobody believed me by the time Saturday arrived but by 2 o'clock I had a big leg of pork in my hands. I won first prize in the raffle!

"As before I announced to the world that I would be winning the National Lottery that week. Already I had been quite lucky and had won four out of five first prizes at our church's raffle. A few days later I hit the Jackpot."

"Craig told me all about this story during the consultation and there's no way he could have known as I'd won. But he told me that I'd win again. And I'm sure he's right."

We'll keep you posted.

Most people fear death and when we lose someone we love the greatest insult to their memory is refrain from talking about them for fear of upsetting the bereaved. But when a medium makes contact with the after world it is rarely a sombre occasion. There are no darkened rooms, no spooky castles or creaking walls. The 'dead' like to prove to us left behind that they are happy in their new life and sometimes pull our leg and joke with us. When a spirit enters the other world they are shown the mistakes and errors of their life on earth but their basic personality doesn't change very much. Often the objective of their communication is just to let us know that the suffering of their passing illness is gone and that they are still the same person we know and love.

One of the main reasons people say they come to see us is just to know that the one they love is all right. They may remember the terrible ordeal that the one they loved went through on their death bed or seen the personality changes that drugs and brain illness brings. After such terrible things could they possibly be made whole again when they enter the afterlife?

It is wonderful to know the truth that once the spirit is free of the physical body a feeling of health and harmony returns almost instantly. However some spirit may need a little help after passing over and are taken to a place known by Spiritualists as The Halls of Healing. Here the trauma of transition and the residue of illness from earthly life is finally dissolved. Life long illnesses may take the spirit doctors a little while to cure but cure they do. In time the spirit person is brought back to the natural harmony and health that is their essential nature. The paranoid schizophrenic finds peace, all bodily ailments disappear and the crippled walk- even fly.

Rosemary Stokes from Winchester in Hampshire nursed her desperately ill husband Ray for 18 months at home. In time, as his condition and pain became intolerable there was no choice but to take him to a hospice. Ray had cancer. He was terminally ill. "It was a terrible ordeal" says Rosemary "He was in a lot of pain and very frightened. We loved each other so much and I used to sit by his bedside wiping the tears from his eyes. To see that dreadful pallor in my loves face was awful. He had been such a handsome and dignified man but slowly everything was being taken away from him. We were living a nightmare yet when he was finally passed away on the 31st January it was a terrible shock even though I'd had plenty of time to prepare myself."

In March Rosemary heard about my work as a medium "Perhaps Craig would be able to communicate with my beloved Ray?" says Rosemary "I'd never had proof, but in my heart I believed that there's an afterlife. All I wanted to know was that Ray was all right."

"Craig told me that Ray was showing him a gold signet ring with a black stone. It was broken and I should get it mended and wear it. Absolutely nobody knew this. Craig told me about Ray's sense of humour and that he said 'Didn't I really look the part all dressed in blue' We buried Ray in a blue suite. He mentioned how he'd met up with his friend Joey who'd only died two years before, how he wasn't insured and how we'd planted a rose tree in his memory. Together they were raising their glasses of Bacardi to me- it was the only alcohol Ray would ever drink. And astonishingly Craig went on to say that Ray was telling him about how when he was in the coffin my daughter had pinned a gold heart onto his lapel.

"To me it was like winning the lottery. Craig said all about the terrible suffering that Ray went through but that like Ray I should put this memory in the past. I needed to let go of those dreadful memories of his illness and know that my Ray was no longer in pain. Although he'd been frightened when he died Ray said that the fear vanished as soon as he saw his father come for him to take him into the better world in which he lived now. I came away from the consultation feeling a lot, lot better."

It's good to know that the one you love is all right and safe in a new world. But some spirit communicators are more than all right, they are ecstatic in loving their new found world. So when Jan Hartnet from Basingstoke in Hampshire visited me, as some people say, 'talk to the dead' the last thing she expected was to be splitting her sides with laughter. "Craig opened by asking if I knew a man who had passed over called Charlie who came from Limerick in Ireland. Of course I did- he was my much loved uncle. Craig added however that although everyone called him Charlie the name on his birth certificate was Joseph which was absolutely right."

"Craig then said that Charlie was telling him that he'd died of a chest complain during the month of September but that Charlie was such a joker that it was going to be hard to keep a straight face.

"Charlie said about how, now that he was dead, his wife would have nobody to nag at- she should have had him stuffed- which was exactly Charlie's type of humour. He said that I was deluding myself sitting there because there was no afterlife! 'There's nothing here at all- don't bother coming' he joked."

By this time we were falling about with laughter as Uncle Charlie fired joke after joke at Craig. "But this was exactly as Charlie was" continues Jan "He couldn't open his mouth without saying something funny."

"Craig stopped the consultation for five minutes so that we could compose themselves then continued. He asked Charlie to give some real proof that it really was him. 'He tells me that your brother is a fireman.' said Craig Your dad was a bingo caller and that he's just had a major operation but is okay now. He says that you've a daughter called Laurie and she has four interests in life: boys, music, boys and music.' We started to chuckle again at the last comment. But Craig was absolutely right.

"Craig also said that Charlie was joking about my car's exhaust pipe- on the day I visited Charlie in hospital before he died the exhaust fell off my car. It was another thing he'd pulled my leg about.

"'You shouldn't drink so much' said Craig 'Charlie says that you should stick to tea like he did.' Charlie was a constant tea drinker. Craig started laughing again. 'Oh my God!, he's just said, mother's going to loose her purse yet again! Mother had lost her purse only days before and shortly after the reading she lost it again. 'You should know this. Last week you bought yourself a set of Tarot cards- but you don't have a clue how to use them!'"

During the consultation Jan also spoke to her sister who told her that she was looking after the stillborn baby she'd lost and that she'd been trying to let her know this by surrounding her with the song of children. "Strangely enough," continues Jan " every morning when I woke up I'd hear children's voices but could never fathom where they'd been coming from."

Charlie's message to Jan was that no matter how gloomy life looks there's always a bright side. "Laughter was just the tonic I needed at that time" says Jan "Sometimes I now dream of Charlie on his bike and wake up feeling cheerful. Charlie told me that life for me was going to get much better- and it has."

Hampshire based school teacher Pam Dibble, 45 loves kids. When Pam's 11 year old daughter Charlotte died from an asthma attack she was devastated.

Charlotte had already tried to contact her mum. 'After she died the light in her room would flicker and on one occasion her cassette recorder started playing by itself" says Pam "It was a recording Charlotte had made of her playing the keyboards. I checked the machine and there were no batteries in it!

"When we moved house I went into Charlotte's old bedroom just to say 'good-bye.' I turned the light on and the bulb exploded with a loud bang leaving just a bare, burnt, dangling, wire. Call it coincidence if you like- but for me that was Charlotte saying a last good-bye."

It was Pam's mother who made the first link from the other side when we began the sitting at her Fareham home. She had already been around Pam and clearly had been preparing the lines of communication.

One of the first things that Craig said to me 'I've your mother here showing herself stood by a wardrobe. And, it may seem odd but she's holding a new set of towels.' This immediately made sense. Only a few days before I was surprised to find, in the wardrobe, a brand new set of towels that had been hers.

'Craig told me lots of correct things about mum such as having water retention in her legs and getting fat even though she couldn't eat towards the end. Craig said that mum wanted to remind me of a funny story that no medium could research in records. She was laughing, said Craig, as she told of how she had lost her false teeth while leaning out of a train window. This had been a long standing family joke- she lost them as Craig had said and remained toothless for two years. She was buried without dentures."

Once mum had broken the ice I could turn to more serious issues.

"It was Charlotte who I really desperately wanted to contact" says Pam "Craig said that he saw her by me holding a teddy bear 'There's something odd about the teddy' said Craig 'It was buried with her ...but there's something missing'. Charlotte was indeed buried with her teddy. It had a missing ear.

"What convinced me it was Charlotte was when Craig said that she was now singing 'The Owl and the pussycat went to sea'. Just before she died Charlotte had done a beautiful illustration of the Edward Lear poem. It had won first prize in the school competition. On the same day that she was being buried her sister collected the school prize on Charlotte's behalf."

One of the reasons that this sitting was so precise was because Pam's mum was able to break the ice by making her laugh about the funny story about the false teeth.

The story was no doubt encouraged by my spirit helpers who work with me and organise the people communicating on the other side. If there's a funny story about false teeth my spirit helper will make sure it's communicated. I think he finds it fun and it does lighten the atmosphere.

I remember telling one lady that her 'dead' father was laughing about the fact that she put his false teeth in her handbag and had taken them with her to his funeral. She told me afterwards that there was a panic on the day and she had rushed to the undertakers with dad's false teeth so that he could be buried with dignity. She was too late so put them in her handbag and secretly carried them with her throughout the solemn proceedings.

Reuniting dead children with their parents has been an important part of Jane's mediumistic work too:

When Pauline Bennett's only son had a fatal heart attack only yards from her home in Totton it seemed to her that everything was lost but Robert soon let mum know he was all right. "I saw him in his bedroom. He just stood there smiling at me. People said it was just my mind playing tricks but I saw him as real as you or me."

Pauline's belief that her son continued in a new life was confirmed when she and her husband had a 'reading' with Jane.

"The first person to speak to me from the spirit world was a friend of the family who Jane correctly said was a German nurse" says Pauline. "She was helping Robert from the other side. When Jane spoke to Robert she gave excellent proof, his name, date of passing and the like. And Jane said how pleased he was that we had bought a memorial garden seat in his honour.

"She also described how Rob had been buried wearing his yellow football shirt and even gave its number. About three quarters of the way through the reading there was a voice in the room that we all heard clearly. 'Mum' it cried out. We were all dumb-stuck to hear Robert's voice.

"Jane said that Robert was concerned about our friend Natasha who was about to undergo open heart surgery. Jane said she would concentrate every night and send her some absent healing. The doctors really couldn't believe what they were seeing. Natasha recovered from her operation in record time."

When I first started working as a medium it used to worry me a great deal if some of the information I was saying was wrong. Sometimes your own thoughts do get muddled with those being projected from the spirit world but more often than not its information that the sitter doesn't know about that they have to verify later.

Jane and I believe that its the evidence that needs to confirmed by a third party that is the most important as it proves to us that what we're doing is not mind reading.

"When Craig said that he was in touch with a man named Frank who died in his sleep I realised that he was talking about Dad." said Jackie Lucas, 38, from Winchester, Hampshire. "What convinced me was when he explained that he had been reading a war novel by Wilber Smith just before he died- which was exactly right. Craig said that he was now feeling happy over in the other world and that he had met up with my step-father Earnest who had died in terribly tragic circumstances. He described events that even the closest of our family don't know about.

"But there were things that Craig said that just didn't make sense. He kept saying that Frank and Earnest shared a love of cricket and that they would talk about it at the pub all the time. Craig said that dad had even lived near a cricket ground. This was news to me but I did know someone who had lived near a cricket ground. 'I'm not referring to George' piped up Craig 'He lived in a flat overlooking the Oval in London- I'm talking about Dad's interest.' Craig was right about George but I was sure that he was wrong about Dad and Earnest."

Jackie decided to check out the details with her Mum. Jackie's Mum had very much wanted to attend the sitting but had backed out at the last minute- the tragedy of her husband's death was still to painful to think about.

"Mum confirmed that years ago, when they owned a pub, Dad and Earnest talked incessantly about cricket and their house at the time overlooked the school cricket grounds in Winchester."

Jackie's mother was also able to confirm another story. "Craig had said that there was a funny family story about Dad losing money over some chickens. Well, he got that right too. One year dad had decided to buy a load of chickens to fatten up and sell at Christmas for a profit. But when it came to the time to kill them Dad just couldn't do it.-He had to pay someone the profits to do it for him."

Mum shed a few tears when Jackie told her the things that Dad had said to prove that he was all right in his new life. "I nearly didn't go to see Craig" said Jackie "I was afraid that I'd burst into tears at the mere mention of

Dad. But it helped Mum and me tremendously. Just to know that Dad's his same humorous self is enough. I'm glad I went"

Jane's mediumistic evidence of survival can be just as accurate:

"Mummy, I've just seen Jamie in my bedroom" said three year old Mike to his mum Debbie Stuart. The psychic tot's night visions were of thirty two year old James Percy who had died a few months before. "He would have long conversations with my dead friend" says Debbie "there were things mentioned in his cheerful, one way conversation that Mike could never have known about."

The first time that Debbie went for a sitting with Jane, Jamie Percy made himself known. "I was only expecting fortune telling," says Debbie," but Jane said that a man named Jamie was trying to communicate through her. He wanted to reassure his mother that he was all right. 'He died of a massive heart attack at work' Jane had said 'and he's showing me the docks and is carrying bags of cement....no it's not cement; it's bags of flour!"

Jamie had died two weeks before Christmas from a massive heart coronary outside the Rank Flour Mills at Southampton Docks. He was unloading flour from his lorry. Debbie passed the message on to Jamie's mother Joyce Percy from Fawley in Hampshire.

"The first thing that Jane said to me" says Joyce about her sitting that Debbie also attended "was that she saw him with a bunch of red roses. 'Is there a wedding anniversary soon' said Jane. In fact it was Arthur and my anniversary the next day."

Jane continued with the subject of flowers. "She then said that my mother was with her also and she brought freesias- they were her favourite flowers. Also she said 'Jamie is talking about crocus bulbs. You're not to plant anymore on his grave. There's far too many of them now.' When I had gone on my regular visit to his grave a week before I had been surprised how many crocuses there were on the grave. It was absolutely covered in them. In fact we had planted one lot too deep and subsequently planted a second lot. Both came up this year and now, as Jane had said, the grave was overrun.

"Jane went on: 'I see a man like the racing driver Graham Hill....is there something about racing cars...no not racing cars Banger cars?"

Joyce explained to me that her son had been a well known Banger racer. She showed me, after the interview, a video tribute that Matchams Park Racing from Ringwood, Hampshire had made for her. It included Jamie's races and the two minutes silence that the stadium had requested from the normally noisy crowd. There was complete silence, James Percy was clearly a much loved and respected young man- over three hundred attended his funeral.

"Jane said so many other things to me that proved beyond doubt that she was indeed communicating with Jamie" continues Joyce "She saw the pair of shoes of his that I still kept, our oval locket of his hair that was cut just before the burial, his love of music (she said correctly that they played 'There is a green hill far away at the funeral) and talked about Jamie's son Sam (from a previous relationship) who we had unwillingly lost touch with. Jane also described Jamie's friend Sid who she said regularly visited the grave together with his little dog and how he used to have to buy endless curries for his girl friend at the time. She said that he was holding a cake shaped like a kitchen sink that I'd made and that at Easter I'd be making another very unusual cake. She could hear the song 'Twinkle, twinkle, little star'".

"For a joke Jamie had asked me to make a kitchen sink cake for his girlfriend as she was constantly complaining that she was forever stood at the kitchen sink. And Jane's prediction about new cake came to pass. I am a helper at the local play group- another fact that Jane picked up- and for the Easter draw they asked me if I would make a cake in the shape of a giant yellow Easter egg. The school children were singing 'Twinkle, twinkle, little star' when they asked me!"

Jamie's father, Arthur, who has been a down to earth milk farmer for forty two years, admits that he was at first very sceptical when his wife told him about the sitting with Jane. "On the evening after Joyce spoke to Jane I clearly saw a figure in our room. There was a cold chill and it walked through the door. I took to be Jamie" he says with a strong country accent, "In the morning we received a telephone call from Debbie. 'Little Mike says that Jamie won't be visiting our house anymore' said Debbie 'He's gone over to visit you instead."

Sometimes people are surprised by my bad memory. When they talk to me after a public demonstration of mediumship they realise that I have forget all the things I said only moments ago. The reason, I believe is that if we mediums were to retain all the memories of death, illness, and heartache that the spirit world show us then it could cause us severe psychological anxieties. Instead, we are a channel for the communication. The impressions come and go. They are washed from our thoughts as soon as they are spoken.

6 EVIL SPIRITS AND THE OUIJA BOARD

"Four of you will die" spelled out the Ouija board. Lis Glen' stepson Lee was 17 when in 1988, for a dare, he and four friends decided to experiment with an Ouija board.

"When Lee told his dad Ken and me he was going to die, we thought he was joking," recalls Lis.. "We had no idea that he and his four friends had been messing with an Ouija board."

About a week later Lee was dead. He was attacked on New Year's Eve when during the fight his head was banged against the pavement several times- and since then two others, who used the board, have died in tragic circumstances.

"Lee collapsed a few days after the fight whilst baby-sitting for my other son's children" continued Lis "He was rushed into hospital and put on a life-support machine. We were told he was suffering a delayed reaction to the bangs to his head and that he'd be severely brain-damaged if he came out of his coma. But on the tenth day, pneumonia set in and he just slipped away.

"A few months later, one of the other boys caught pneumonia while camping and died. It was a shock as he'd been so healthy.

"That's when one of Lee's other friends came to see us. He was in total panic and told us about the Ouija board. It all seemed so ridiculous to us," reflected Lis. "But this year, another of the group took his own life, leaving only two out of the five."

Lee's passing was a terrible blow to the whole Glen family. Not only did they suffer the shock of Lee's passing but there followed an inquest and the awful prospect of an inquest on Lee's body. His dad found the pressure too much to bare, there were arguments in the family and he gradually sank into a deep depression. Lee must have seen all this from the spirit world. He tried to make contact:

"A few weeks after Lee died, strange things had begun to happen to us." says Lis "One time, Ken and I were watching TV when we heard footsteps upstairs. We thought we were being burgled- but when we checked, the room was empty. It really scared us.

"And that was just the beginning. Another night, I put the kettle on and then left the kitchen. When I came back, it was unplugged and on the other side of the sink from where it normally is- and it was cold, despite having been boiled once already. Then a picture that had been hanging in the hall for years fell off the wall for no apparent reason.

"We also started to lose things and, despite turning the house upside-down, we never did find them.

"Even when we moved house this year strange things happened. Ken was making an aviary and a pot full of screws and nails completely disappeared.

"We began to wonder if it was Lee's way of trying to keep in touch, and decided to look for help. It was then we heard of mediums Craig and Jane Hamilton-Parker......"

Lis and Ken came to see Jane and myself at a Mystic Fair that we were staging at Ocean Village, a leisure venue at Southampton Docks. Lis had a reading with me and at the same time Ken went to Jane's table close by. Lis had overcome her grief but Ken was still suffering from severe depression- he told me later that it had become so bad that he was even seeing a psychologist for help. The psychologist apparently said that Ken seeing us had been therapeutic.

Lee seemed to be communicating to us both simultaneously

"Jane did a reading for Ken and attempted to tap in to Lee. She said things that only Lee and Ken could possibly know- that Lee's motorbike had been traded in for a CD player, and that when he dyed his hair it was a funny colour- he'd dyed it just before he collapsed.

"Jane and Craig have told us the strange occurrences are Lee's way of saying he's okay. Until we met Jane and Craig we'd known nothing but sorrow- now I hope we've reached the turning point."

Was the death of Lee Glen really predicted by the Ouija board, or was his and the two subsequent deaths more a case of coincidence and self-fulfilled prophesy? Methods of spirit contact like Ouija boards are subject to all sorts of influences that may not be spirit people at all. Jane and I are inclined to believe that the 'occurrences' around the house may be Lee's way of trying to communicate but perhaps other mental powers influenced the board. "This is an exceptional case" explains Jane, "but I don't honestly think the attack on Lee can be connected to the teenagers' sitting around the Ouija board."

The Spiritualist Newspaper, *Psychic News*, asked Eileen Roberts, president of the Institute of Spiritualist Mediums and lecturer on mediumistic development, about the case and how easily the subconscious mind can govern Ouija board messages.

"This could have been a genuine communication warning the teenagers, but we are generally ignorant of the many things the mind can do," she said.

"It is easy for susceptible people, especially teenagers, to be emotionally upset by such a message."

Although she admitted that the attack on Lee was unlikely to be any kind of self-fulfilled prophesy, she speculated there may have been elements of this in the other two deaths.

"All you need is for one person to believe such a prediction and it sparks off others," she suggested. "Perhaps the boy who caught pneumonia on the camping trip decided he was going to die anyway and felt less inclined to resist it. "For a trained medium the Ouija board can be a legitimate method of spirit-communication but because the general ignorance about how they work is such that I often feel like gathering them all together and burning the lot."

There is an interesting postscript to this story. About a year after Lis Glen had her consultations with us, a young lady called Jackie S- came for a sitting with me. Immediately I had to tell her about her brother, a young man with the name Richard, who died on St Valentine's Day from pneumonia. I described how he was a bit of a rebel, had a sarcastic sense of humour, could be lazy and smoked roll up tobacco like myself. He joked about himself and I felt him urging me to reassure his sister that he was all right and hadn't changed much since he passed over to the spirit side.

'My death was predicted' I heard Richard say. 'I was one of the lads who played with the Ouija board with Lee. Tell Alan that he'll be okay. He'll have a long and happy life.' I repeated what I was told to Jackie who by now was in tears. When we had begun the sitting I had no idea that Jackie S was connected through tragedy with Lis Glen's family.

The next day I contacted Lis Glen's son Alan. When I mentioned the Ouija board incident he visible shuddered. But when I went on to give him Richard's message it was as if the burden of years of worry was lifted from his shoulders. Alan now runs a successful printing business. He's happily married and I'm sure will one day will be a very prosperous man.

In the right hands the spirit communication methods of Ouija boards, plachettes and table tilting are quite safe. But it's so very important to make sure that the work is done in an atmosphere of love and sincerity. If this vital ingredient is missing then chaos results:

"For twenty years I have kept quiet about the frightening things I saw" says Di Spotiswood (60) from Waterlooville in Hampshire, "But now I feel I must speak out in order to warn others of the dangers of playing with Ouija boards."

"It all started as a game when some teenage friends of mine started using the Ouija board. An old man who once owned the country bungalow in which the séance was being held started to communicate through the board. Other neighbours became interested in what was going on and soon quite a crowd would visit to watch the proceedings.

"But the language used became abusive and foul- which amused the 'players' who answered back with similar tones. I was called in to help when things started to go very badly wrong.."

"Everybody blamed everybody else when swear words started to appear on the walls. But there was no arguing when articles started whizzing through the air and narrowly missing the small children.

Incredibly wardrobes moved around as though they were made of matchwood, voices were heard, bumps and bangs sounded all through the night- and the whole family became absolutely terrified. I saw burly, muscular men tremble with terror on seeing these things.

"The worse thing I saw myself was the unshaven face of an old man push through the kitchen wall. I saw it happen. It was as plain as day. And as it happened I felt a burning sensation from head to toe.

"I spent hours on the phone trying to track down someone who could help us. Finally I managed to find a medium brave enough to go along. She identified a young 17 year old girl as the source of the energy that fuelled the poltergeist activity. The medium's involvement helped but the bungalow never completely returned to normal. The family eventually had to move.

It has often been known for poltergeist activity to be centred around teenagers in puberty and the medium may have been right in identifying the 17 year old girl as the source of the activity. However it is more likely that the crowd of participants fuelled the poltergeist with negative psychic energy. For centuries the Tibetan yogis studied this and called these entities Tulpas. They can cause havoc for a short period but inevitably, given time, their energy dissipates and the activity ceases.

When John and Joyce Allen from Wootton Bassett in Wilts moved into their house the last thing they expected was to be transported into a series of events worthy of a programme from the X-Files. "It all started 10 years ago when items in our house started to go missing and were returned in another location." says John "There was no logical reason to explain what kept happening. It wasn't caused by absent mindedness or children and pets carrying off the objects- there was no logical explanation.

"Soon we discovered that my neighbours in the Crescent were all experiencing similar things. In particular, the house two doors along saw items flying around, electrical switches switching themselves back on, a piano playing by itself, a dog was heard and items flew through the air and even around corners.

"Most people in the crescent assumed it was the ghost of a lady called Anny Moody and her dog, who used to own the old 'Canal Wharf House Inn'. It was a house of ill repute at the turn of the century and was demolished in 1982. Many claim to have seen Anny's ghost walking our street.

"I did some research and discovered that the houses were build directly on a ley line which is where 'earth energies' are said to accumulate. And the house where the poltergeist activity happened was build exactly on the intersection of two major leys. As far as I could discover, there had only been one death in the crescent since the 1950's.

"The ghost of a small boy with callipers was also seen by myself and many people. He had died, he told us, during the 1st World War and was looking for his father who had been killed in France along with 20 others in the Flanders fields. I was unable to trace the boys address in the records."

After 3 years of strange paranormal activity John and Joyce had had enough. "I called in our local Spiritualists to assist the trapped spirit people to move on into the other realms." says Joyce "I sat with them in the séance and I have to say it was a very strange experience indeed. I felt the pain and suffering of the various soldier's wounds as they communicated through the medium.

"We concluded that the soldiers and a Second World War pilot were trapped by the energy of the ley line and the crippled boy with his dog had been trying to attracting our attention to help free his friends.

"The Spiritualists now appear to have exorcised the ghosts and buried various crystals around the area to disperse the ley line's energy. John did some further research and the soldier explanation appears logical. The houses in the Crescent were once owned, I discovered, by the MOD."

Parapsychologists have found that many of the most famous poltergeist cases have happened at the intersection of two ley lines. These are said to be a network of earth energy lines that criss-cross the country. The prehistoric inhabitants of ancient Britain were supposedly aware of these lines of force and built their monuments on the most important concentrations of these fields. Stonehenge is a prime example.

I am aware that the events caused the family severe distress which resulted in many problems. Persistent earth bound spirits can be very disruptive and it's often the Spiritualists that get called in to sort matters out.

It is unusual for Spiritualists to identify the source of a haunting as the node of intersecting ley lines but times are changing. I believe that their diagnosis was right. The earth does have areas of negative energy where nasty elemental powers can accumulate. Many people now believe that these negative areas are places where 'Earth Rays' that rise up from the centre of the earth are distorted by underground streams and rock strata A negative 'geopathic' area will make a person feel uneasy, tired and tense. Because of this some places just don't feel right and can even cause illness for people who inhabit these places.

As well as centring on areas of Geopathic Stress the energy required for poltergeist activity and vivid haunting can accumulate because of water. In some cases underground streams and covered wells supply the energy. In this next case it may have been the sea herself:

A committee member of one of our local Spiritualist Churches telephoned us one evening to explain that they had a problem. "A lady has contacted the church and claims that she and her husband are being attacked by a poltergeist." said the Spiritualist. "Someone or something has been throwing objects around the cabin of their boat on the Solent and, she says, it has also been attacking her. We sent along one of our local mediums and he feels that this is a real phenomena and not just a figment of an overworked imagination. He felt, however, that it would be best if a strong group of mediums could be assembled to tackle the problem together. He is convinced that it is real as there's a strong and violent presence onboard. Would you two be prepared to help?"

The occurrences happened mainly at night we were told, so this would be the best time to have our séance. Jane and I agreed to go along and a date was fixed for the following Saturday night. There would be five us taking part - We'd have enough psychic power between us all to make a serious challenge to the poltergeist.

It was on the Friday night before that we realised that this was going to be a real case of a haunting. Something happened that shook us both.

Jane and I were laying in bed talking about our plans for the encounter the next night. We were both relaxed and feeling quiet, peaceful and at ease. Our conversation was interrupted when the room lit up with an intense blinding white light. We both sat bolt upright in bed. My immediate thought was that it was lightning but the weather forecast had already predicted that it would be a clear evening with no threat of thunderstorms or rain.

And it most definitely wasn't lightning. There was a second brilliant flash and the room remained illuminated for some time. The light then folded in on itself and formed into a luminous ball about four foot across in the centre of the room and floating at about head height.

Jane and I sat speechless as it hovered for what seemed like an eternity but what in reality must have been about thirty seconds. It then shot across the room, out of the door, and toward the living room. I leaped out of bed and gave chase. Seconds later it disappeared leaving no trace.

Jane and I had seen things like this before but never with such an intensity. As a young child I would experience a ball of light that seemed to read my thoughts- a manifestation of spirit perhaps? Jane had a peculiar experience one day whilst alone with her then nine year old daughter Chantal from her first marriage.

"Chantal and I saw a ball of orange light about a foot across hovering in the living room" says Jane "It moved towards us and hovered in the air about three feet in front of us. Chantal was becoming frightened as I put my hand out and tried to touch it. My hand went straight through it. There was a swishing sound as the ball of light bounced onto the TV and out of the window."

Jane and I had never seen anything as brilliant as that Friday night's manifestation however. We were both, to say the least, startled by the experience but we didn't feel that we had encountered anything malicious indeed the room felt peaceful with a sense of well-being.

It did effect us physically though. We both felt sick, there was a sickly scent in the air, we were sweating, and our solar plexus region felt uncomfortable- as if it was knotted. I have read of similar reactions in physical circles, where the mediums manifest ectoplasm, although Jane and I do not claim to be physical mediums.

Surprisingly, the whole experience startled but didn't frighten us. We believed that a spirit from the higher realms had visited us to reassure us that we were well protected and to prepare us for the next night. The angels were looking after us.

It was already beginning to get dark when we met the other mediums who would be going onboard the boat. This was the time when the owner of the boat said that the spirit was most active.

The old converted fishing boat looked ominous and creepy against the darkening sky. It creaked and groaned as it rocked with the tide. The sultry evening was turning colder and across the river we could see the lights of other boats bobbing up and down. The moon was casting its first rays on the indigo waters.

We kept the mood light by joking between ourselves. With this type of situation its best not to be too sombre and serious.

Jane and I had spent some time before in deep meditation to prepare ourselves and had by now opened our psychic awareness. The lady, who was having the problem, was clearly troubled. Her aura, we could see, was full of prickly sensations and dark colours. Our initial task was to gently question the lady to see if the phenomena were the product of her imagination. She and her husband appeared to be honest. Soon we would find out for certain.

"Watch your head as you go below" said the husband of the lady as he guided us aboard. The spiritualist banged his head.

"And watch yourself round here" he banged himself again. We all chuckled. It was important to keep a cheerful light hearted spirit between ourselves as we prepared ourselves for the encounter.

We all squeezed round the table at the bow of the boat and settled down with a nice cup of tea. The atmosphere onboard was odd but not as sinister as Jane and I were expecting. It was certainly a strange place to live and not a place for those who loved their creature comforts. There was limited decoration, a lot of damp, and no space at all. It had a musty smell. "Perhaps" I thought "the lady is using the excuse of a haunting to get her husband to abandon these unfeminine conditions for a brick built home on land."

Once we had settled in we all relaxed and tuned-in to spirit. John ,the medium who first organised the clearance would, we all agreed, act as the leader of the group. His wife Ethel sat next to him, Jane and I sat together and Nick the church member sat opposite us. The husband and wife who owned the boat stood in the doorway to the side of us. A prayer was said to ask for protection and for God to be with us with our work.

"Father may you give us the protection that we need with this work. Bring to us from spirit those guides and helpers that we each know and also those that come here to help with this type of work in particular. May the higher angelic helpers be here with us also. Protect us in what we do and give your blessing to our task so that the troubles that fill this place may be lifted. Amen"

As the words of the prayer unfolded we could feel a strength and joy as the power of the spirit built around us to aid us with our work. The next step was to challenge the spirit to come forward. Like a snake under a dark rock we had to coax it into the light and disarm it. The boat was still but some of the keys hanging on the wall on a nail swung a little. We all noticed it but continued as if nothing had happened, perhaps it was nothing.

"Come on, you coward." said John in a loud stern voice "You've bullied this lady enough! Now there are five of us to take on. Come on, we challenge you to show yourself. Come out!!"

Nothing happened. Again he made similar retorts. "Come on ,show yourself. You want to scare people, come and scare us!"

Then we felt, what can best be described as a thickening of the atmosphere and a feeling of someone stood close to us. I could feel the face of a man press close to mine then leave me and went towards Jane:

"The man felt angry and very violent yet at the same time he felt frightened and confused." says Jane "I could tell that he didn't like women at all and that he felt it was bad luck that women should be on his boat. "Get away from me "I projected in my thoughts "Go and pick on a man, you bully, go and try and take on Nick from the Church"

As Jane sent these thoughts we all saw Nick's face changed. His went bright red and he looked frightened.

"Who's he with now "somebody said aloud.

"He's with Nick, can't you see" I said.

"That's right he's over here with me "said Nick. We all sent out our power to help Nick with his struggle. The spirit left him and I felt him draw close to me. I closed my eyes and said:

"There seems to be two of them, there's a little boy here with an angry man, someone has been hit hard across the head with something heavy. That's one of the things that's making him so angry."

"I felt it across my head as well" said John, "And me too "said his wife Ethel. He has a thing about women being on his fishing boat. It's bad luck!"

The spirit man's unexpressed anger at the time of his passing was holding him to this world. His death was linked somehow with a woman and he was taking it out on the lady that now lived on board.

We all agreed that we were feeling the same sensations and description of the man in spirit. We countered his anger by all mentally projecting thoughts of love and encouragement for the trapped soul to progress onward to the spirit world.

"Come on now" said John, "Your time now is finished. It's time to go to the spirit world"

We felt the spirit moving between us. His aggression began to soften. I felt him leave Jane and the others and return to me. I could hear his voice clearly in my mind.

"I'll suffer for what I done if I go over there" he said in a rough rasping voice "They'll send me to hell for sure"

He drew closer still. I tried to reassure him that no God sat in a golden throne was going to throw him into an eternal hell. God didn't want vengeance he wanted only our love. Hadn't this man suffered enough by being bound by his anger to this world. He owed it to himself and the young boy who clung to him to seek God's unceasing forgiveness. He had as much right as anybody to enter the kingdom of heaven, his own conscience would be the judge of his soul.

As each of us reaffirmed these ideas in our own way we could feel the spirit man's grip begin to loosen. We all sensed him crying. He let go. The ecstasy in his soul was contagious. As he departed I had a beautiful vision of a great staircase leading up through the clouds with angels of light stood at the sides. I could see the man's silhouette small and dark against this heavenly setting. I was seeing that man's image of heaven as he left this earth. Perhaps when I die I will have a different passing vision but what I saw that night was quite beautiful. Another soul had found peace.

The heavy atmosphere had left the room as we all started to return to normal consciousness. The suffocating atmosphere had gone.

"He's gone now" Nick said to the lady "Can't you feel the difference in this place?"

The boat was, as far as we know, never troubled again.

The people who approach Jane and I come from all walks of life. We've seen doctors, solicitors, businessmen, and even a high court judge. But when a psychiatrist telephoned and asked for assistance I was very surprised- normally they reject mediums out of hand.

Warminster based psychiatrist, Dr Medway, contact me and asked if I could visit her patient's home to find out if it really was haunted. "The lady involved is convinced that she is under a ghostly attack." said the psychiatrist "She insists that a poltergeist is throwing things around the room and that a shadowy man is trying to attack her."

We visited the house together hoping to convince the lady that there was nothing to worry about. But when we stepped into the living room we all saw a strange white mist that clung to the floor. It was clear that we were dealing with something real after all.

The lady showed me around the house and I sat and meditated at the places where she said the manifestations were strongest. I described a bearded man who was troubling her. The description fitted what she had been seeing.

The spirit told me that he was a gypsy and that he was buried nearby. I talked to him calmly and after a long and difficult inner debate he agreed to go. The psychiatrist looked as relieved as everyone else.

When the records were checked it was found that gypsies had camped extensively in that area many years ago. They had no formal cemetery but it was believed that they buried their dead in the vicinity of the house in the woods that had once covered the estate.

It appears that many of the spirits that supposedly become trapped on the earth plane have worries about their place of burial. For example, Julie Benyan's family from Horton Heath Hampshire have a recurring ghost. The family live in adjoining cottages. 'Problems mainly occur in granddad's house." says Julie "Sometimes there's an mysterious burning smell that's followed by a rap on the door. Nobody is ever there. The whole family have heard unexplained footsteps and we often hear loud raps from the coal house."

Julie believes that two ghosts haunt the house. They researched it's 100 year history and found out about a epileptic boy whose parents used to lock him away for days in the coal house. "This may account for the coal house rappings " says Julie "But we also learned that a terrible murder took place here in Victorian times and a body was buried in a ditch outside. The murder is still unsolved so perhaps the ghost is still trying to communicate and tell us what happened"

In the case of Beverley's family that follows next they were at first scared of their ghost but now treat her as a family friend:

"All our family have seen the little Victorian girl who wears a long night dress- we have called her Emily. I asked the previous owners of the house if they'd seen anything and they exclaimed 'Oh she's back again is she?" says Beverley from Hampshire.

Jane was the first to investigate Beverley's story. "My first impression was that Beverley had found Emily's blue patterned jug in the garden and I pointed out where Emily's dog's grave had been" says Jane.

Beverley confirmed that bones and blue china had been found where Jane said. Jane said that the girl had died in the well that they had recently covered over. They later checked the records and found this to be true- beneath the new kitchen was the remains of an old well.

When I investigated the cottage Emily told me about a St Christopher medal the owners had found under a tile in the kitchen. I pointed to the stone tile and they confirmed that this was the exact place it was found. Beverley rummaged through a draw and handed me the St Christopher to help me build my link with the spirit by holding it.

Emily took me on a tour round her old home. She was aware that she knew that she was dead but preferred to stay put so long as nobody minded. It was her that had been trying to draw attention to herself by moving the children's toy clowns and, as described and witnessed by Beverley their mother, making them come alive. Beverley decided to burn the offending clowns in the garden. "There was a piercing scream as I threw them on the bonfire" said Beverley, "It nearly scared the life of me."

Emily was sorry that she had scared them all.

Jane had got it right when she visited earlier. She'd told the owners that Emily had fallen down the well when the authorities arrived to take her to a children's home after her parents died. Children's homes in Victorian times were fearsome places.

The spirit of Emily began telling me how the house had changed and the owner was able to confirm this. Strangely one of the bedrooms had once been a larder and Beverley said that they'd had to completely strip this large room of wooden shelving and cupboards. The children's room, I said, had once been Emily's and this is where I was told she had most often been seen dressed in her long white night dress.

There was one manifestation of Emily that had not been so pleasant. Beverley told me that on one of the walls on the house a marking had appeared and disappeared.

Emily led me into the living room and told me to place my hand on a particular place on the plain, clean wall. "It wasn't a simple mark" I exclaimed "It was a red hand of blood"

Beverley looked shocked and I began to wonder if I'd spoken out of turn. I didn't want to be alarmist but, although she'd said nothing about this to anyone before, this is exactly what the whole family had seen at the place where I put my hand. Again I could feel Emily from the spirit side apologising.

"Although some people would be worried by a ghost we feel that Emily is a nice spirit to have around" says Beverley "She's never given us any more trouble and the last thing we would want is for Craig & Jane to get rid of her."

Stories similar to this are often sent to me at my newspaper columns or when I write for the women's magazines. This next one really intrigued me, not because a real ghost was involved, but because the whole family seemed to be so genuinely pleased to know that their house was haunted:

Nobody knows quite how old the traditional Somerset Farmhouse of Willow Farm adjoining the site of this week's Glastonbury Festival is. Some of its stonework, and particularly the stone pillars by the fireplace, was retrieved from the ruins of Glastonbury Abbey that was destroyed by Henry VIII. Legend has it that long ago two brothers jointly inherited it but argued incessantly. Finally a blood-bath took place within the house as one brother brutally murdered the other.

You won't be surprised to know that the farmhouse is haunted.

"The whole family is aware of our ghost." says Jane Fear (57) who together with her husband David brought up her four children in the house. "It was my eldest daughter Sandra (31) who gave it the name Freddy. "

"Having a ghost around the house was part of our childhood" says Sandra "So many spooky things happened around our house that we all take it for granted. The strangest occurrence is when my brother Richard's (34) bedroom door open and we hear footsteps cross the landing and walk down the stairs. When it reached the bottom we would see the stair door open by itself.

"When this happens one of us will usually call out 'Oh Fred we do wish you'd learn to shut the door!'"

"We've had the occasional visitor been terrified by what happens." says Sandra's dad David "They have refused to stay in the house but we see no reason to worry. Fred's never hurt any of us and even our 3 dogs and three cats seem comfortable when he's around."

In 1976 the main beam of the house gave way and considerable work was undertaken to repair the house. "We were all worried that Fred would either clear off or show his disapproval when the repairs were complete" says Sandra "Mum was really concerned. But within a few days we saw a shape at the top of the stairs and the doors and footsteps were soon back"

"I was overjoyed" says Jane "It would have been awful to lose Fred- he's part of the family!"

The Fear family certainly don't live up to their name. They take exactly the right attitude. Many people are absolutely terrified by the slightest creak or hint of a ghost. Sometimes ghosts are just an atmosphere left in a building that replays itself like a video recording. Sometimes a spirit gets trapped between this world and the next and they are usually more frightened than we are. I'm sure that the attitude of the Fear family to Willow Farm's ghost will help Freddy to progress toward the higher levels of the afterlife.

Another great story sent to me involved a very spooky country ghost known locally in Malmsbury as The Green Lady:

'It was October 1954 and I was 24 years old. My glorious grandmother, who I adored, was dying. I thought of her as I cycled home to Malmesbury on the road between Crudwell Village and Lord Suffolk's Estate. There were a couple of cottages to my right and opposite was a farm gateway. As I approached it I saw an apparition gliding about 4ft in the air and drifting towards the centre of the road.

It was a misty Sunday morning so I assumed at first that it was the light playing tricks on me. I cycled up close and came face to face with the figure. It was a woman in a long brown coat. She had a featureless face with dark, empty sockets for eyes. Not knowing what to say or do I stuttered out the words 'Good Morning'

As I spoke, the silent figure floated slowly backwards into the gateway. I was more curious than frightened.

For years people laughed at me when I recalled this weird event. But my husband listened and in 1963, soon after we married, we visited the same place and asked at the cottages about the ghost. 'You saw the Green Lady who haunts that very spot!' replied the householder. On the Tuesday after seeing the ghost my grandmother died.'

This story was sent to me at one of my psychic columns for the newspapers. It is a good example of what we call a ghost, phantom, apparition or spectre. Some people are mystified, intrigued, shocked or frightened when they 'see' this form of spontaneous phenomena.

There are scientists believe that the brain emits an electrical 'morphic field' that imprints itself on the environment. Ghosts and apparitions are seen when our psychic abilities read these mental recordings. Consequently the same ghostly figure is seen time and time again at the same place. The lady's fatigue from cycling and her sensitivity at the time of her grandmother's illness probably opened her to these vibrations. Just as we would say that a photograph of a person is not the person themselves so a ghost is likewise not a conscious being. It is a series of mental vibrations left in the atmosphere of the environment that a sensitive person can perceive unfolding like a film. The case you read about the ghost train in an earlier chapter may be explained in this way.

In the case you read about the boys playing with the Ouija board it is debatable whether spirit forces were present at all. When a group of people gather to consciously manifest psychic phenomena they can tap their own mental powers which influence and manipulate matter. Scientists call this power psychokinesis. When the young men assembled around the Ouija board their thoughts blended together by telepathy. As they asked about the future their subconscious fears were triggered and the result was the frightening prediction that became self fulfilling. When I spoke to the dead Richard for his sister he indicated to me that spirit entities were not involved in their terrible game.

The stories about the haunted boat, the gypsy graveyard and the Victorian child called Emily, I believe were manifestations of conscious spirits that were 'earthbound'. When the time of death comes, the spirit and the physical body part company. Manifesting in the etheric body the spirit goes on to a different dimension to our material world and joins the afterlife. Feelings, memories and personality are retained by the spirit.

Earthbound spirits are those that, for various reasons, still cling to our world. Often they do not even know that they are dead. An unresolved inner conflict, feelings of revenge, guilt or a desperate need to finish their earthly business stops them progressing. These spirits cannot hurt or harm anyone- they have no body to hurt you with- but may frighten some people. Mediums are trained to link with these entities who wish to make contact and will reassure them and help them to move on. We will send out thoughts to direct the departed one towards other spirits who know and love them and together convince the earthbound spirit to enter the ever forgiving afterlife.

Although it makes interesting reading, work with earthbound spirits is only an very tiny part of our work. Cases like these are extremely rare. The main thrust of our mediumistic work is to communicate with the spirit people who return from the bliss of the afterlife to reassure their loved ones on earth that they are happy, safe and well.

7 DEAD CELEBRITIES MAKE A COMEBACK

Most entertainers are creative, extrovert and sensitive - the same personality traits that paranormal researchers tell us makes a good psychic. So it's no wonder that the superstars of the creative professions have paranormal tales to tell that are stranger than Hollywood fiction. Some claim to know the future, are in touch with the dead and even posses the power of spiritual healing.

For example, pop megastar Michael Jackson claims that he inwardly communicates with the flamboyant, pianist Lee Liberace who died in 1987

"I have my own secret room, with a moving wall and mirrors" said Jackson, "that's where I talk to Lee. His is the voice I hear in there. I feel his presence so very close to me." He added that Liberace "is like my guardian angel. He's even given me permission to record his theme song 'I'll Be seeing You'."

Liberace also believed that at times he was paranormally inspired. He owned the piano which once belonged to the classical composer Liszt. "When I play his compositions on it I have the most eerie feeling, as if I'd played that music before in another time." And just like Liberace, Lizst was a flamboyant dresser.

Some musical stars have deliberately sought the advice of the spirit world. Rock star, Roger Daltry of 'The Who' says he spoke with the band's former drummer Keith Moon who died of a drug overdose in 1978. "I've spoken to Keith, or rather to his spirit," says Daltry "There's a psychic woman I go to see who doesn't know who I am or who Keith is."

Pop star Neil Tennant, from the "Pet Shop Boys" also spoke to the dead and saw his future with the Ouija board.

"It happened when I was 15, a group of us decided to have a séance, and we got in touch with the ghost of Oscar Wilde. He warned us not to make the same mistakes that he did. He told me I would be famous one day"

Neil was pleased with the news from spirit "It was the advice I was longing for. "Ever since I was a young lad, I desperately wanted to be a pop star."

Creative people often have latent powers are more inclined to see spirits and ghosts. Mick Jagger, lead singer for The Rolling Stones, was spooked by a bell ringing 18th Century ghost when house hunting at a £3.5 million Gothic mansion. "He seemed to change his mind rather suddenly after we told him about the ghost" housekeeper Anna-Maria Sliwinski told reporters. "I have heard the ghost first hand. I heard strange chimes on a windless night. The bells were ringing in the tower, but there was nobody else in the house."

'Ghostbusters' actor Dan Ackroyd even claims to be haunted by his best friend and co-star John Belushi who died of a drug overdose in 1982. He claims to see Belushi in Studio 8H where they worked together. "It's weird," says Dan Ackroyd, "It's as if John is trapped in limbo there."

Singer and TV star Cilla Black knows what it's like to share your house with a ghost and has often seen the spectre of a girl by her bed. "She's appeared to me loads of times." says Cilla, "She's about 14 with a sweet, sensitive face that has a really sad expression. I had this strong feeling she was searching for someone."

Researchers revealed that a man called Thomas Redley once lived in Cilla's house in Buckinghamshire, England.

His wife died suddenly and soon after Thomas died of a heart attack. Their daughter Lillian was left in the house alone. Three years later she died from pneumonia, aged 13.

The ghost of Lillian appears to be quite friendly but no so the poltergeist that haunts the house of pop star and actor Sting. A mysterious power sent a razor sharp knife flying across his kitchen. "It propelled itself over the room and embedded itself into a wall" says the singer "Just before that, the mobiles in my daughter's bedroom began to spin crazily although there was no one in the room at all, even all the windows were tightly closed so there could be no draught whatsoever."

Sting or his daughter were probably displaying the powers of psychokinesis which is defined as the power of the mind to influence matter. This psychic energy can move objects and in some people manifests as a spiritual healing power.

Again, Liberace believed he had healing powers. "Why, the other day , in the Hollywood Bowl two cripples arose and walked at my command. I said to them. 'If you really want to walk for me, you can!' So they did."

"I have never professed to be a faith healer but the incidents referred to actually happened."

Soccer legend Pele- hailed as the greatest footballer ever- says he can cure cancer-stricken children and help crippled youngsters walk again. He told Brazilian Playboy magazine that he performs miracles when parents ask him to visit their children. "Those children are in wheelchairs." he says "Miraculously, when I touch them they start walking again- my God!

"I visit them in hospital and the boys and girls are cured.

"Parents call me saying their kid has one month to live. I go to the hospital and the kid recovers."

Many stars have experimented with spiritual healing when they've been taken ill. Michael Bentine, voice of the Goons, is today fighting bone cancer with the help of spiritual healers. Bentine's father was a psychic researcher and it's not surprising that his son should follow in his father's footsteps.

Film star Omar Sharif was more sceptical. While filming in Bulgaria he was doubled over with pain because of a stomach ulcer. Then the producer's wife, actress Betty Bolvary, told him that she was a spiritual healer.

"At first I scoffed at her", admitted Omar, "but she insisted, asking me to give her just one minute. Gripped by pain, I thought, 'What will one minute cost me? So I agreed."

After Betty had finished, Omar Sharif had changed his tone: "I realised in that moment that the pain had gone. There was not even the slightest twinge. In 60 seconds I had been cured."

Many psychics and healers believe that crystals, and particularly quartz, can amplify healing energies. It has been claimed that Elizabeth Taylor's persistent health problems may be caused by her love affair with over powerful diamonds. Crystals are said to have protective properties as well.

Actor Michael York is a firm believer in ESP and takes an interest in the New Age movement that is spearheaded in the United States by actress Shirley MacLaine. He believes that a pocketful of crystals saved his life when six thugs attacked him and his wife in Rio de Janeiro. The actor went to defend himself and to his amazement the muggers fled. He is convinced that the crystals, which were given to him by a Brazilian healer, protected him.

Gloria Swanson, who passed away in 1983 also accepted the reality of spiritual healing. "I have seen healer Miss Kuhlman cure dozens of people of many different illnesses." she said when interviewed by American broadcaster Bryce Bond "I have seen little children become hysterical with joy when their mothers or fathers suddenly walked after years of being crippled."

"I accept the afterlife's reality" she also said and described how once she left her physical body and "went a few blocks away"

Like Gloria Swanston, many psychic believe it is possible to leave the physical body or clairvoyantly witness events taking place at another place. The American chat show hostess Joan Rivers has claimed to have travelled out of her body. She says that she 'flew' to California, where her daughter lived. "I saw my daughter in the shower- I rang immediately to confirm what happened- and that's exactly what she had been doing."

Mediums, like myself, believe that at physical death the spirit leaves the body to enter the afterlife. But that's not the end of the story. The people we love can return to guide and inspire us through our intuition. Hollywood heart throb and star of the hit film Ghost, Patrick Swayze says he is frequently visited by the spirit of his father who passed in 1982. "He appears in my dreams as an old Indian warrior. We were so close. I still want to cry every time I think of him," the star comments.

Jane Fonda, daughter of late movie star Henry Fonda also claims her father's spirit visits her. Jane says of her famous dad who passed in 1982: "I welcome the interest he takes in my work. After all if anyone should know about the movie business it's Henry Fonda."

Many people get a psychic flash of foreboding that can sometimes save a life. Actors and actresses are no exception. Actor David Niven's wife Hjordis had a premonition that she would be accidentally shot. On one believed her even though twelve guests at a shooting party heard her comments.

"Sure enough," said one guest, "our host didn't see her standing behind a bush and accidentally shot her. Fortunately she was at the edge of the pattern of shot so she was not killed. Hjordis got 30 shots in her."

Singer Eartha Kitt believes that her ESP gifts are a "strange power which can suddenly warn something bad will happen to someone very close to me." In 1965, whilst visiting Argentina, she sensed that something was terribly wrong with her three-year-old daughter so she took the first flight back home to Los Angeles.

"I hurried home to hear my daughter cry 'Mommy I'm so sick' She had a temperature of 103 and was rushed to hospital where she fully recovered."

Earthers warnings have proved correct in several instances. When, in 1955, she greeted her best friend James Dean, Eartha told him "Your body is here, but your spirit isn't." The young actor passed seven days later in a car crash.

Actress Ursula Andress didn't like the vibrations she felt from the car either saying "I told him the car gave me a bad feeling. He promised to be careful and said goodbye. I knew I would never see him again"

Many famous stars such as James Dean have believed in an afterlife or had premonitions of their death. Elvis Presley said that he believed he would die when he saw pictures in cumulus clouds that predicted his death. In particular John Lennon, of the Beatles, took an active interest in Spiritualism and attended many séances with his wife Yoko.

It is believed that John had a premonition that he would be shot. He even stated that his fear of murder caused the Beatles to break up.

"We were not bored," he said, "and certainly did not run out of songs. I was paranoid about somebody trying to bump us off." When he heard that the Beatle's road manager had been shot dead by Los Angeles police he said over and over again "I'm next, I know it."

But John believed firmly in an afterlife. "I am an optimist about eternity. I believe in life after death. I believe that death is not an end but a beginning."

Many world leaders are also deeply interested in the paranormal and ESP. And their beliefs may have influenced their military decisions. President Jimmi Carter believes he saw a UFO and Ronald and Nancy Regan's interest in astrology has been well reported. Biographer Kitty Kelley claims that when Mr Regan became California's governor in the late 1960's he took his oath of office in the middle of the night "acting on advice from an astrologer who said that this was the most propitious time."

The author also claims that the Regans "were devoted clients of Carroll Righter, a Los Angeles astrologer, and secret devotees of Jean Dixon, a 'seer'." It is claimed by many sources that President Regan always consulted the stars before making his decisions- a tradition that Hillary Clinton is maintaining.

President Mikhail Gorbachev's paranormal interests are less well documented. However, it was alleged that, before he fell from power, he smuggled a blind clairvoyant called Vanga into the Kremlin so she could 'read' sugar cubes for him. The troubled Soviet leader was said to have "quizzed her for two hours on his future" before flying her home to Bulgaria in a government aircraft.

When questioned about the incident a Kremlin spokesman said, "It's no secret that Gorbachev has been under immense strain recently and this prompted his actions."

Considering the events that soon followed, I expect that Vanga's predictions were far from sweet.

In Britain, it was Queen Elizabeth I who first made major political decisions based on the evidence of 'seers'. Her clairvoyant advisor, John Dee was a secret code number: 007- the same secret agents number adopted by Ian Fleming for his fictional spy, James Bond. Dee prophesied the attempted invasion of England by the Spanish Armada in 1588 and the execution of Mary, Queen of Scots in 1587.

Paranormal beliefs had enormous influence on strategic decisions and world events during World War II. Hitler, Himmler, Goering, Rosenberg and Goebbels' interest in the occult is well documented. Hitler was born in Braunauam-Inn, Austria - a place known for its seers and magic traditions. As a young man he was taught to develop his psychic abilities with Professor Haushofer and later in Vienna attended numerous lectures about numerology, graphology, water divination, astrology, psychokinesis and physiognomy. One of his early associates said that Hitler believed that he could detect Jews by dowsing over them with a pendulum and the Nazis applied phrenology to determine who had Slav, Jewish, Bolshevik or Aryan sculls.

A distorted version of the prophesies of Nostradamus, who predicted the rise of an anti-Christ called Hister, was used by the Nazis for propaganda purposes and Hitler consulted his own personal astrologer Karl Ernst Krafft when making major military decisions. Realising that how Hitler's war strategy was being influenced by metaphysical considerations Churchill in turn employed his own astrologers to ascertain what decisions Hitler was likely to make based upon the movements of the planets.

Sir Winston Churchill, the man of destiny, possessed a natural psychic gift himself that saved his life many times. In his autobiography he says that in his youth he had held a planchette "and written while others had touched my wrist or hand." He also tells of how in the Boer War, as a reporter for the *Morning Post* his train was ambushed and he was confined to a prison camp.

He escaped into territory unknown to him but says that his intuition guided him to recklessly knock on the door of a house and reveal that he was British.

"Thank God you have come here" cried the stranger, "It is the only house where you would not have been handed over. But we are all British here."

His life was saved again when fighting in World War I on the Western Front. While he was with the General, his dugout was blown up. He said later "And then there came the sensation that a hand had been stretched out to move me in the nick of time from a fatal spot."

During the blitz, clairvoyance saved his life again. Churchill always sat in the same seat in his car but one night suddenly decided to change his routine. A bomb landed nearby and he would have been killed if he hadn't made this impulsive seating decision.

When his wife asked him why he'd made the change he said "Something said to me 'Stop!' before I reached the car door held open for me. It then appeared to me I was told I was meant to open the other side and get in and sit there- and that's what I did."

In 1940 he again sensed danger and in his mind's eye 'saw' the huge windows at Horse Guards Parade, which backs onto 10 Downing Street, being smashed. He ushered everyone to safety three minutes before splintering glass sprayed the building.

Churchill believed in destiny and that some invisible power guided his life "I have the feeling that we have a Guardian because we serve a great cause, and that we shall have that Guardian so long as we serve that cause faithfully."

Across the ocean, Franklin D Roosevelt was being guided by spirits. There is strong evidence to suggest that he attended séances. A 1944 edition of *Chimes Magazine* said that he and some of his cabinet "secured very good mediums, held many séances and listened carefully to suggestions made by former presidents, generals, admirals and diplomats now residing in the spirit world."

In Canada, William Lyon Mackenzie King, who held office from 1935 till 1948, was also consulting the dead. He made no secret about this to his intimate friends, some of whom joined his séances in his library at home. King used both the crystal ball and a Ouija board and his diaries reveal that he experienced visions and prophetic dreams.

On his death bed heads of state gathered to meet him including King George VI, Churchill, Pandit Nehru and two strange unknown women. The two women sat with him for 50 minutes as he made his preparations to die. They were Geraldine Cummins and Miss Gibbes- an Irish medium and her companion.

In Russia, Stalin was also taking an interest in the paranormal. When he heard of the astonishing psychic abilities of the Polish Jew Wolf Messing he decided to meet him. The perplexed Messing was arrested and questioned by Stalin himself about the destiny of Russia.

Stalin decided to put Messing to the test. He was to undertake a 'psychic bank robbery' and take 100,000 roubles from the Moscow Gosbank, where he was unknown.

Wolf Messing could use his telepathic powers to hypnotise. He walked into the bank and handed the cashier a blank sheet of paper and was immediately given the money he wanted. Two of Stalin's official witnesses confirmed to their leader what had happened. When the cashier realised that he was holding a blank sheet of paper he fainted with shock.

As if this wasn't enough, Stalin demanded that Messing undertake another impossible task. He took Messing to a secure Government building and personally ordered the three guards insisting that Messing, under no circumstances, should leave the building. Messing succeeded again and cheekily waved good-bye to a high government official looking out of one of the windows.

But Stalin still wasn't satisfied. Messing must risk his life again. He was ordered to illegally enter Stalin's heavily guarded country house. Messing used mental suggestion to convince the guards and servants that he was really Lavrenti Beria- the head of the secret police even though he bore no physical resemblance to him. Once again he triumphed.

Stalin was so impressed that as a reward he granted Messing permission to tour freely throughout the Soviet Union- But, he could probably have used his psychic powers to do that anyway!

And finally, even the devout Roman Catholic Charles de Gaulle joined in WW 2's paranormal pursuits. When France fell to the Nazis he fled to England to lead the Free French fighting forces. Here he consulted the British medium Bertha Harris who he met at a country house party. The other guests included Winston Churchill and King George of Greece- a firm believer in Spiritualism.

Bertha predicted that de Gaulle would liberate France and that he would become its leader. The prophesy was fulfilled. Charles de Gaulle lead the French troops into Paris in June 1944 and later became his country's President.

8 FLIGHTS INTO THE SPIRIT WORLD

"Craig said that he was looking for a lady in the audience with the name Jenny who understood the surname Mathews." says Jenny Perrin from Poole in Dorset about the message she received from me during a public demonstration I was giving of mediumship.. "'This was a recent passing.' said Craig ' It was a young, somewhat rebellious man who died before his time.'

"Another lady in the audience thought it was for her but Craig soon understood that he was on the wrong link. He realised that the message was meant for me. I took the surname to be of nineteen year old Brett Mathews- a very close friend who had died a few month ago. We had known each other since early childhood and were like a brother and sister. I was still suffering from the shock of his sudden and tragic passing.

"Craig explained that Brett was a soul who was not meant to reside on earth for a long time. Everybody complained that he had died before his time, but really he had come home; he loved his new life in the afterlife.

"'He's explaining the way he died' continued Craig 'It's pitch black when the tragedy happened. Something hit him so hard from behind that it even broke the sternum of his chest. Others were with him when it happened. They were caring lights. I believe that he's telling me that he was struck from behind by a train'

"Craig had got it right this was exactly what had happened on that fateful night." explains Jenny.

"Craig continued by describing some of the other things that Brett was showing him: how he continually ate chewing gum and couldn't stand still, rode a bike, had a recent girlfriend called Joe, how he cheated at cards and that he had got the letter from his friend Peter. Craig also said that Brett was talking about someone called Keith Jenkins who was grieving for him. He mentioned the games we played as children and how we used to own an oil lamp with a picture on the front of it and a strange roof like shape on the top. As children we also adopted a Jack Russell dog. He gave the birthday dates of June 14th and September 9th as being significant.

"Craig had again got it right but was wrong with the birthdays but then Brett never was much good at remembering birthdays. The numbers were the wrong way round: Brett's birthday was the 14th September and mine was the 9th June. Craig also kept saying that he could hear the word 'Street' but couldn't hear the place name before it. 'Street' wasn't a road at all. Brett must have been trying to tell Craig about Kelly Street, one of his closest friends who was torn apart on hearing the news of the death.

"Brett was trying to reassure us all that he was all right in the afterlife. Craig said that Brett's mum was taking his death very badly and he wanted her to know that he loved her. 'You've seen him twice yourself' said Craig 'on one occasion the door slammed and he says, in his own words, that it scared the shit out of you!!'

"That's just how Brett would have phrased it. I'd seen his figure in my bedroom twice and on the second occasion the wardrobe door closed by itself. I nearly leapt out of my skin."

Brett Mathews had reassured his friends that he was all right and told many things about his life. But perhaps one of the most important things he didn't say in the communication.

An important fact that didn't come through in the communication from private Brett Mathews was that this young man from the First Battalion Devon and Dorset Regiment based in North Germany had died bravely. The incident had happened on on a Monday in January during night manoeuvres. One of his comrades had got his foot caught in the railway line and it was Brett who had sacrificed his own life trying to save the life of his pal.

There will always be a place in heaven for heroes.

"We didn't expect that evening to also get a message from our close friend Martin Cooper" says Jenny's mother Linda Perrin (44) from Poole who had only just started taking an interest in Spiritualism, "but when Craig, at the same clairvoyant demonstration, said that he had an impatient and quick tempered man communicating with him and calling himself Cooper, I put my hand up. Nobody else could place the name so it appeared to be for me and Simon who was sat with me.

"Craig continued by saying that Martin threw all of his money away before he died and that he was joking that he didn't believe in an afterlife and still doesn't now. (Martin in life had called Spiritualism a load of baloney) His death he told Craig was sudden and he had died in a shop doorway. He was stood up but fell to the floor banging his head as he did so.

"Martin Cooper (46) had been a drug addict. He spent everything he had on drugs, sold all of his possessions and ended up on the street. Despite everyone's efforts, and believe me he was loved by many people, there was nothing we could do- he hated himself and was determined to destroy himself. His body was found in a shop doorway in Boscombe Sovereign Centre near Bournemouth. His head was bruised.

"Craig went on to correctly describe Martin's other physical ailments such as the arthritis in his right hand, his stomach condition and that he had a fear of cancer of the stomach. Martin mentioned the watch that Melanie had. It wasn't working. (We checked this out later and the watch had broken down a couple of days before)

Craig described what Martin's mother was like and said that Martin wanted to let everyone know that he is all right now. 'Stop worrying and know that I'm happy in the next world.' There was a lady in Lancashire who still hadn't heard the bad news yet said Craig. Her grief was to come. (A very close friend of Martin's lived in Oldham, Lancashire but was still away on holiday in Tenerife. She hadn't heard the news.) 'Also', said Craig 'He's telling me to make sure that his scrappy dog is looked after.' Martin and his girlfriend Jean had a poodle dog whose coat had got very untidy. Jean had given the dog away to friends.

"We all really sat up when Craig concluded his communication. 'They're shaving me' Craig said that Martin was telling him 'Just a minute, he says that they're shaving him right now. At this very moment. He's not been buried yet! His body's still in the morgue!!'

"There is no way that anybody could have known this. Martin had only died the day before and they were preparing Martin's body as Craig spoke.

At the time of death the 'astral body' of a person, which is like a body of light, leaves the physical body and ascends to one of the heavenly planes. It is unusual for the spirit person to be able to communicate so clearly after the time of death although I've interviewed many people who say they've seen the recently deceased soon after they've passed over and even attending their own funeral!

Many medical doctors are convinced that there is a consciousness that can exist separately to the physical body. When some of their patients come close to death or has a traumatic accident descriptions are given afterwards of being able to leave the physical body and observe what's taking place in other locations. The next casebook is a good example:

What started as a family outing shopping for antiques became a nightmare for pregnant Melissa Pauper and her family. As her husband Richard drove her and their ten year old daughter Samantha back to their home in Dorset they were involved in a head on collision. The combined speed of impact when the two cars collided was the equivalent of hitting a solid brick wall at 85 mph. All three passengers were left unconscious and trapped within the crumpled car. It took over two hours for the fire brigade to cut them out.

"Immediately after the impact everything went totally quiet and calm and we all became aware of being engulfed in a soothing yet brilliant ice blue light" says Melissa (37) "It seemed to surround the whole car. Even though I had multiple injuries -I'd broken my sternum and fractured my spine- I felt nothing. Richard had gone through the windscreen and Samantha had serious head injuries. There was so much carnage that, as far as I knew, everyone was dead.

"I then found myself outside of my body and sitting at the side of the road on a low flint wall. The wall was like a divide. Behind me was this beautiful green field. There were no trees just a big green plain as far as the eye could see. It was so peaceful, so beautiful. In the field I could see people. They were of all ages and all dressed in white. I could see children playing. Everyone was laughing and joking. The sky was clear blue and cloudless.

"In front of me, on the other side of the wall and where the accident had happened, there was no colour at all. As I looked in the car I could only see Richard. It was as if I was standing back watching someone else's accident.

"Then, out of the blue light, stepped a petite old lady and a grey haired old gentleman. I felt that I knew them somehow. They put their arms out 'Join us. Come and Join us' they said. I had an overwhelming urge to follow them into the beautiful green field.

"But a voice pulled me back with a jolt. 'Mummy don't go!'. It was Sam. As soon as she called me there was a painful wrench and I was pulled off the wall and into a tunnel. Suddenly I was back in the car and in a lot of pain. .

"Afterwards Samantha told me that she had also stepped out of her body but couldn't get to the wall. She had been circling the car in a daze then found herself back in her body and cried out to me. I wonder whether this is why I only could see Richard in the car when I 'saw' it."

"As well as being worried for Sam and Richard I was of course also worried for my unborn baby. We had been trying for so long to conceive and we'd made all the preparations and had started buying baby things. As I drifted in and out of consciousness in the ambulance I was visited by another spirit person, a small bald headed man in a tweed coat and round glasses. He looked at me with a knowing smile and laid his hand upon my tummy. I understood at that moment that he had come to take the soul of the baby into his keeping but that she would be given back to me"

Four months later, Melissa lost the baby and was told that because of her injuries she could never again have children. "I was devastated by the news, as the thought of having a baby was keeping me going." says Melissa "But part of me never gave up hope. I remembered the angelic spirit messenger who told me that the child I would loose would be given back."

On Christmas Day 1995 she fell pregnant and on 27th September 1995 gave birth to Annabella who is now 22 months old.

"Bella is a very spiritual child." says Melissa "It's like she's been here before. She wakes up laughing, rarely cries and is happy all the time. If any person can read my thoughts it is her. If I want her to put something down that she's not allowed to play with she'll drop it as soon as I send her the thought."

"The accident has awakened something inside of me. I was always a little bit psychic but now these powers have become very strong. It's taught me that material things are unimportant and that what really matters is life and people. I am now more aware of other people's feelings and have an uncanny knack of being able to anticipate people's thoughts and feelings. I'll just come out with things and they'll be right."

But the most remarkable psychic talent that Melissa has learnt from her ordeal is that she can now step in and out of her body at will. "I can astral travel deliberately. If I loose something I'll sit down and relax and be taken straight to it. For example, the other day I lost my watch. I sat down, relaxed then found myself behind the wardrobe in the bedroom. When I went and checked, there was the watch exactly where I had 'seen' it."

NEAR DEATH EXPERIENCES

The studies made by researchers such as doctor's Sabom, Kubber-Ross and Moody of testimonials from hospital patients who have been snatched from the brink of death demonstrate that many people report similar experiences- they step outside of their body into their astral form. From a vantage point, usually on the ceiling, they see their 'dead' body. Sometimes they recall, when resuscitated, of having seen their operation in progress. They narrate details about the procedures that, without an extensive medical knowledge, they could have never known. One of the most remarkable stories was told to me by Elizabeth Fratton whose story I wrote about in a popular woman's magazine.

Elizabeth Hyde from Fratton had a severe asthma attack and was rushed to the old Royal Hospital in Portsmouth. "I vaguely recall waking in an oxygen tent and a lot of fuss going on around me. I don't know at what point I drifted out of my body but I do know now that my heart stopped and I was rushed to the Resuscitation Ward. I could see myself attached to a ventilator with lots of wires connected to me. I could see a doctor, two nurses and the bizarre sight of a man dressed in a bow-tie and full evening suit!"

Elizabeth then went into cardiac arrest but witnessed the unfolding scene fro outside her body. "I saw them all trying to restart my heart. I was in no pain and felt no difficulty with my breathing. I was an onlooker, so to speak, watching myself in the hospital bed.

"We had no telephone at home and I saw the police bring my husband to the hospital. 'Is there any hope?' I heard him say. 'Very little' replied the man in the evening suit. That was the only moment I felt unhappy.

"I felt myself falling down a tunnel and saw my life flash before me like a rapid series of camera pictures. Suddenly I was standing and feeling wonderful with a sense of lightness, happiness and knew that I was surrounded by a great love. Added to this was a feeling of tranquillity. I felt so well it was wonderful!

"I then found myself stood to one side of a small arched bridge. There were people singing, not hymns but a lovely song of joy. There were colours such as I have never seen. I wanted to join them but thoughts of my husband stopped me. There were also things that I still wanted to do in life such as have a baby- but it was so very, very tempting to cross.

"Stood on the bridge was a Jewish man holding a cross. He 'spoke' to me telepathically and asked 'Are you ready to cross?' I recall saying 'No. No No!' then immediately returned to my body. I could now 'hear' conversations going on around me in the hospital. 'She's slipping away' they said. But I knew that I would live and started fighting the ventilator to prove that I could breathe by myself. 'Why can't these people see I'm not going to die?'".

After four days Elizabeth was detached from the ventilator, transferred to a recovery ward and gradually got well. "The man who previously wore the evening suit when I was in a coma was now in a doctor's white coat as he walked into the ward. I asked the nurse about him. 'He's the surgeon who performed a tracheotomy operation on you to try to save your life' said the nurse. 'I know' I replied 'But why was he wearing a bow-tie and evening suit?' The nurse was dumb struck and then explained that they had to call him from a very important dinner engagement!

"I did have a child- a son, Simon who is now 27. The pervious year I lost a baby but I know he lives on and one day I will see him. I know I am lucky to have had such a wonderful experience."

"Perhaps psychic gifts run in our family" says Simon "Mum and I will try to call each other at exactly the same time. I know that Mum's experience helped her when Dad died as she now convinced that there's an afterlife. As for me, I used to regularly see his spirit walk into my room when I was a little boy."

Elizabeth's story is one of the most amazing accounts of a near death experience that I have ever been told. The sceptics will of course still say that it's all hallucination but how could you have possibly have known that your surgeon was wearing a bow-tie and evening suit? She was in a coma and having a tracheotomy performed. Liz also knew that it was the police that brought her husband to the hospital, she overheard their conversation and knew that a doctor and two nurses tried to resuscitate her heart.

I am also intrigued by the fact that you were greeted into the afterlife by a Jew holding a cross. Perhaps this tells us that the afterlife is not the exclusive domain of any one religion?

Most of us have heard of the tunnel of light that dying people have described. They are drawn through this after leaving the body and are met, on the other side, by radiant angelic beings and by the 'dead' friends and relatives who they once knew and loved.

But they are barred from going further across a symbolic bridge, gate or door when a being, usually a loved one, tells them in gentle tones that it is not their time to die. They are instructed to return, a prospect that has little appeal, and find themselves instantly transported back to the pain of their earthly body. Having tasted the nectar of heaven and glimpsed the ineffable beyond their new life goes through a spiritual metamorphosis. This material world, to which we are bound, seems pale compared to the glories of heaven. They long to return to that ethereal place that is our true home.

And that's the account we have so far. A tantalising glimpse for the subject and a frustrating incomplete story for the rest of us. The critics propose elaborate theories to dismiss these testimonials. They point the finger at the hallucinations created by the drugs used; to the disassociation resulting from the firing of the brain's temporal lobes, the fantasies of a brain starved of oxygen, effects of the release of brain's natural opium like chemicals and the illusory visions created by left brain hemisphere activity.

These alternative theories are, in my opinion, inadequate. Often the patients are free of drugs, we don't know the function of the temporal lobes, ingested opium doesn't automatically trigger an out of body experience and memory recall, when the brain is starved of oxygen, is absent or at best fuzzy. The Near Death Experience is vivid, lucid and changes a person's life forever.

The evidence we have considered throughout this book points to the existence of the afterlife. The reports of NDE's, the dreams and visions of the dying, the centuries old beliefs of religions, the experiences of hypnotised subjects; taken collectively the evidence is overwhelming.

The philosophical principal of Occam's Razor proposes that the simplest solution is usually the right one. The opposing theories of a few sceptical scientists twist and turn and in some cases border on the ridiculous. There's more evidence to support the existence of an afterlife than there is scientific evidence to support the theory of relativity. Scientists can accept relativity- it confirms their belief in a material universe- but talk of an afterlife arouses deep felt resentment and as much scorn and derision as Galileo's telescope did to the Catholic Church.

Heaven and the Angels

The early mediums believed that the Afterlife had a physical reality made from 'Etheric Matter' that encircled the earth in concentric spheres. This they said was like the matter of earth but vibrates at a much higher frequency. Just as microwaves and X rays are invisible to our perceptions so too this Etheric Matter is invisible to our eyes or scientific instruments. Some still argue today that this etheric matter exists and point to the missing 'dark matter' that the mathematics of cosmology says must be there but which just can't be found. If these mediums' theories are right then science may one day provide the key to unlock the door between this world and the next.

I believe, as do many mediums, that the afterlife should be thought of as a level of consciousness. To scientifically prove it we need a new science: the science of consciousness. But an empirical study of consciousness may be impossible: As the Zen masters explain "The mind is like a sword that cuts but cannot cut itself"

But what is consciousness? Is it measurable? Does it have a substance? What is its relationship to the concept of the self?

The questions raised are conceptual rather than empirical as there is no way, as yet, to measure consciousness. Nobody knows what it is and are at a loss even to begin a systematic study of it. Other baffling questions are raised by its study: Are all living things conscious? Could a machine become conscious? Is an unborn baby conscious? Are we fully conscious or do we also have an unconscious? Is our consciousness dependent on the body? Is consciousness and Self one and the same? And so on....

The light of consciousness is the most perplexing enigma of the universe. Being conscious as opposed to 'dead' is certainly important to us. As far as we know, it is Nature's greatest achievement- unless it's possible for nature to evolve something even more baffling. (Perhaps it's NOT the ultimate achievement of evolution? Maybe there is a state of being or non-being that goes beyond consciousness and already exists or non-exists somewhere in the far flung dimensions Creation?)

Psychologists argue that we also have an unconscious and some propose that the left hand and right hand hemispheres of the brain function very differently and display contrasting forms of awareness. Psychologists generally agree, although there's no final proof, that consciousness is generated by the brain.

But even if one experiment in telepathy or mediumship was accepted as fact by traditional science it would demonstrate that consciousness can exist independent of the brain.. Consciousness would be proven to be independent of matter. And the brain and body would be seen to be the temporary housing in which the spirit lives for five score and twenty years.

If you can accept, without having to depend on faith, that the afterlife is a reality then you must also accept that there is a purpose to life on earth. This temporal sphere is, in my opinion, just a stepping stone to something greater. Material possessions, power, position, status have little value in the plan of things: a shroud has no pockets. We are instead on a holy mission to discover our divinity- the treasure beyond the material that worm and moth cannot corrupt. The search takes place in this life and continues in the life to come.

We are born to this world because there are certain spiritual subjects that we are obliged to learn on our path to Self-realisation. Here is the school where we take the lessons. For the advanced pupil the lessons are hard because they demand that we change ourselves, evolve spiritually and take personal responsibility for our actions and destiny.

Our teachers are many but the greatest of them all is suffering. A spirit forged between the hammer and the anvil in the fires of adversity grows great.

The poet William Blake expressed this in a beautiful way: "Man was made for joy and woe, and if this we rightly know, then safely through the world we go." In other words, it is through joy, suffering and acceptance that we learn our spiritual lessons. To free ourselves from attachment, and earth is the place where the forces of craving are most pronounced, brings liberation. To be free is to learn to love unreservedly. To fly we must let go.

Some of life's lessons appear so brutal and unfair. For example how wrong it appears that a baby who dies only weeks after its birth should have such a limited experience of this world. If this life is the place where we learn the lessons to prepare us for the next then that child is going onto the next world disadvantaged. Surely they would get a second chance to learn the experiences available through life? This is one of the many reasons why Jane and I accept that reincarnation is part of the cosmic plan.

Many mediums do not believe in reincarnation- they say that it is unproved- although numerous spirit teachers, who have spoken through famous trance mediums, say the soul takes on many incarnations..

Reincarnation explains why some people suffer and others have an easy life. To be born into a comfortable life does not necessarily mean that the person involved is worthy or those that suffer do so because of evil deeds done in previous lives. Everyone has different lessons to learn from life. For some, wealth brings suffering and for others, poverty brings spiritual growth. This world is the testing ground for the soul and each of us has a unique, custom made examination to pass or fail. We return again and again until we have fully understood the lessons and changed ourselves accordingly.

But the next incarnation is not instantaneous. We spend some time on earth and also time in the afterlife. When we are spiritually ready to learn new lessons we are reborn, together with those who are part of our group soul who will become our friends and family in our new earth life. The group soul consists of those who are bound together spiritually by a common love and destiny. They will be people on earth who you will instinctively love. There will be other members of our group soul who do not join us this time around- you are yet to meet some of your oldest friends.

Latent in our soul are the buried memories of past lives and of our time already spent in the afterlife. But, as in the Greek myth, we have passed across the river Styx and forgotten our lives from before in order that we can experience the world anew. But one day we will remember.

A simplistic description of the afterlife explains it as a world very much like this one, where we spend an eternity under pleasant circumstances. This 'tea and biscuits in heaven' mentality is rejected by many thoughtful mediums. Like this world the spirit planes are temporary places of residence. The first planes of afterlife existence are similar to this world but there are worlds within worlds in the beyond. Advanced souls, who have understood the illusionary nature of earthly existence, will, when they pass over, enter quickly into the higher more abstracts states of consciousness. It all depends on the discarnate individual's level of understanding.

Entry into the afterlife is experienced in terms we can readily understand. We experience a world that is a perfected version of earthly life. Our soul is free of the restraints of the physical body and we see this level of reality in its full splendour. It is a world that is more beautiful than our own and many souls will continue at this level until it is time to take on another earthly incarnation.

Some souls will continue to live and experience a similar life to the one they knew on earth. Although they have no physical body they may continue to eat food or live in houses and do their chores such as housework, driving a car or perhaps even visiting the launderette! Gradually they may understand that their activities are illusionary habits. As their understanding of the nature of the afterlife increases they will become less dependent on the old earthly behaviour patterns and embrace a more fluid state of being.

When mediums communicate with the afterlife it is through these first planes, that are closest to earthly existence, that the spirit makes his communication. Also, from Jane and my experience, the communicating spirit's personality deviates little from their traits they exhibited on earth. The stubborn and swearing 'Uncle Frank' often cusses and swears and puts bigoted views even when he's gone to heaven. Some express their guilt concerning their earthly behaviour but the personality itself doesn't seem to change a great deal. They become more aware of themselves but do not suddenly become enlightened.

The afterlife, I believe, is made of 'mind-stuff' i.e. consciousness. It is a plane of 'being'. When a person enters the afterlife they take with them the sum total of their understanding. Most people comprehend the world to be something 'out there' and that the external world is real. This way of perceiving is taken with them into the next planes of being and they experience the afterlife in terms that they are used to and understand. Consequently, they enter a world that is very much like this one with towns, countryside, skies and houses. Also they experience the afterlife within the cultural context that they knew on earth. i.e. a westerner will see a western style civilisation.

The major difference between this world and that of the afterlife is that the entrant is now free of the physical body and can experience reality without the constraints of the brain. The author Aldous Huxley thought of the brain as a reducing valve, a prison, that blocks the true perception of reality. He took mind expanding drugs such as mescaline that opened his perceptions and allowed him to see the world in its 'naked existence'. Huxley's ecstatic, psychedelic visions are probably similar to the world we will see with our celestial eyes in the afterlife: incandescent, alive, vibrant and beautiful beyond words. We will see reality in its primal form.

Mediums like Jane and myself, communicate with the afterlife and assimilate information that we pass on to our sitters. Together with our own direct visionary experiences are able to build a picture of what the next world like. Much of what we have to say, and what other mediums have said in the past, is similar to the reports of people who have had a near death experience but for the spirit communicator it must be like trying to explain colour to a person born blind; it's impossible to describe unless you've seen it for yourself.

And there's one thing you can be sure of. One day you *will* see it for yourself.

The Angels

Mediums believe that their work is guided by spiritually advanced beings from the higher realms of the afterlife planes. Like the Bodhisatvas from the Buddhist tradition they return from the bliss of exalted consciousness to teach their message of love to the rest of us. When the medium enters a trance these spirit guides are able to directly communicate with us through the mouthpiece of the medium.

I first became aware of my spirit guides as a young man of 19 and the spiritual bond between us was further enhanced when I sat in Peter Close's development circle. They are now very close to me, often guiding me during times of difficulty and will advise me of the appropriate words to say to my sitters. Without the protection and wisdom of these spiritual helpers a medium's work would be fraught with danger.

For many years I worked as a professional artist and as I put paint to canvas I would become so immersed in my work that I entered a different state of consciousness- an inspired state of creative revelry. Artists often refer to this as being inspired by the Muse but when the Muse started to talk to me I began to wonder whether there was a conscious being behind the voice. At first the inner voice would guide my artistic activities but gradually it started to give me advice about my life. When I followed the instructions it invariably proved to be the right advice which took into account situations that I was unaware of at the time.

Perhaps the voice was my own inner voice? Could I prove otherwise? The voice always gave helpful, encouraging advice but was it healthy to encourage it? I had met a number of schizophrenics and saw at close hand how uncontrolled voices could torment their soul.

The answers to my questions came suddenly and with such force that I could no longer dodge the issue. It was as if the ground fell from underneath me and I was floating in a black void. Before me was a beautiful light so beautiful that I instinctively fell towards it. As I did so I felt my personality being stripped away. Everything I cherished and held dear fell away from me. I knew that what was happening was an irreversible process. If I went with the experience I would never be the same again. I would perhaps no longer exist

A voice called to me across the void. 'Let go! Let go!'. Every possible excuse to resist flooded my mind. With every excuse came the same answer. 'Let go! Let go!' I stopped resisting and did as instructed. I let go of everything that was me and tumbled towards the light. I dissolved into infinity.

It is impossible to explain in words the experience that followed. To say that I became infinite light is not enough for light is of the world To say that I went beyond form is not enough for I was beyond form yet one with it. To say that I became one with God is not enough for the word God has too many associations and limited preconceptions.

I then emerged into a joyful abstract world that had form but not as we understand it in our dimension. Beside me stood a young Buddhist Tibetan monk. 'When everything dissolves, all that's left is love.' he said. He was expressing the words that I found impossible to formulate. 'Are you real?' I asked 'Or are you my higher self?'

He smiled. 'I cannot answer that question, the experience you've just had was real was it not? Does it matter if I'm real or not? Judge me only by the truth that I speak. If I cease to speak truth then please reject me.' A life-long friendship had begun.

Over the years I have now accepted that the monk, who gives the name Taratha, is real. He has spoken through me in trance and given messages that other mediums have confirmed. Occasionally other mediums have even repeated the exact words of instruction that he has spoken to me the previous day. He has told me facts about Tibet that I have been able to check in obscure Tibetan texts and says that one day he will be able to confirm his identity beyond question. I will just have to wait and see, but as the guide said 'Does it really matter. All that matters is the truth of my words.'

Taratha is not my only spirit helper. There are others too and many of these are not on a high plane of spiritual understanding. For example, an Italian clown, who works with me during my public demonstrations, has to be held in check by the other guides. He shows me how to make the audience laugh and so raise the vibrations to make spirit communication easier. His little trick is to press the spirit communicators for stories and anecdotes about false teeth. He's brought forward stories about a lady who carried her husband's false teeth to the funeral and of glorious grandmothers who edged their pies with them. I could write a book about stories of false teeth given as proof of the afterlife!

Each one of my guides has given me subjective and objective proof of their reality. I call them the wingless angels. At my circle that meets every Wednesday evening and has been featured on a television documentary, Taratha talks to the group. I enter a trance that deepens as Taratha takes control. At first I am vaguely conscious of what's being said but within a few moments I lose nearly all awareness of the discourse given. I enter, what I can only describe as, a light headed awareness. I'm surrounded by a peaceful inner light and hear my voice speaking far away. Like a faint, overheard conversation across a crowded room the words are heard but unintelligible to me.

My regular sitters have included a surgeon and two GP's, intelligent people who are not predisposed to fantasy. The reality of the trance is further confirmed when, if the power is high and the trance deep, the guides will allow someone known to one of the sitters to communicate directly through me. They have been able to provide evidence of survival and the spirit communicator is recognised by their voice, gesture and the nature of the private information given to the sitters at the séance.

I will now recount one of these sessions that was recorded on cassette during a period of trance. I was completely unconscious of what was being said during this spirit communication:

A MESSAGE FROM A WINGLESS ANGEL:

'Good evening my friends. The talks I have given you in our discourses so far have all addressed the same fundamental question: What is the nature of reality? My answer is simple. There is only one reality. And that reality is God. You may call Him by a different name, the absolute, Brahman, Allah, infinite consciousness, omnipresent love, limitless energy, the cosmic sea of being, Nirvana but in the end it is all the same. God is One. It is the same God that inspires every religion.

God is both personal and infinite. He is manifest and unmanifest. He is conscious and unconscious. He has form and no form. As you talk to me you can also talk to God in your heart. As I answer your questions so too

God can answer your questions when you look within. For you are a manifestation of God but you are separated from this realisation by ignorance. Matter and the world of spirit are nothing other than the concrete thoughts of God. The quest of life on Earth and of life in the Spirit is to realise your oneness with God, to remove the veils of ignorance.

Like sunlight that shines through a stained glass window, the one reality has separated into many forms. You see only the spectrum of the world before your eyes but there exist worlds within worlds. I talk to you from one of these worlds that lies beyond material form. I talk to you from beyond the threshold of what you erroneously call death.

Your world and the Spirit World are One. It is too easy to think of the spirit world as being separate from your own. But it is not, the two worlds are of the same reality but you are not fully aware of this truth. The same fundamental energy vibrates at different frequencies to create different worlds. The universe of matter is only one part of this spectrum of vibration. In time science will understand this. The world of form is a sluggish vibration where matter can only be manipulated with matter. In the Spirit and the higher planes the substance of our world is manipulated by mind alone. The constant throughout Creation is not material light but the 'light' of consciousness. Awareness exists on all planes of being..

So, you will understand, Energy takes different forms depending on how it vibrates and many parallel world are thereby created. The spirit world, like the world of matter, has form but is more malleable and can be changed and manipulated by mind. Consequently, when a person first enters the Spirit they see a world that is familiar to them; a beautified version of the world they knew on earth. But soon they discover that the Spirit does not have as many limitations as earthly life. Time here does not travel in a straight line, communication is made directly between minds, travel takes place at the speed of thought and perfect worlds are created by mind and limited only by the imagination.

A spiritually advanced soul will quickly see that there are few limitations yet those who bring with them their earthly desires will continue live in an earth-like reality. For many the afterlife is intrinsically the same as on earth: they eat, sleep, live in houses and continue the routines they once knew. But the soul that is inspired by spiritual love will continue to progress. They will see that the work on themselves must continue- even in heaven. Beyond the spirit planes are higher planes still. Planes that they must ultimately progress to. Their heart's desire will be to progress onward, to be liberated from form and personality ultimately to merge with the godhead. Inner prompting and guidance from advanced souls will reveal to them that their goal is to return to the source and become angelic beings. Self realisation comes when the soul no longer clings, when it lets go, when it falls in love with the divine. For love is giving; love is surrender..

In life you have free will but once union with the godhead has been realised your will and God's will become one.

The spiritual quest that I have outlined is emerging today in the hearts of many seekers. The religions of the world can no longer quench the thirst for spiritual truth. Where once words and belief was enough today the seeker wants to know and experience the truth for themselves. You will witness, in the coming years, the bankruptcy and near collapse of religion. As this happens you will also see many environmental, economic and political troubles in your world. But as the old form dies a new light emerges that will illuminate the ancient religious teachings and strip away the self righteous arrogance that has prohibited direct contact with God. Where once there was fanaticism and separatism now there will be modesty and unity.

To bring this change about, many angelic beings from our world have incarnated in human form. They come to reawaken the ancient knowledge that has for so long been lost or distorted. You will see miracles. The bigoted will lose their power and strangle hold on truth as seekers realise for themselves the true reality. From India, Russia, Brazil, Japan, America and Europe the universal religion will be born to transform the world. But it will not be as the religions you once knew. The new religion will be enthroned in the heart. It shall have no form or doctrine yet will animate every religion. It shall not be founded on fear but will express itself as love.'

9 LOVERS FROM A PAST LIFE

You have read stories from our casebooks that indicate that most of us, perhaps all, have ESP powers that enable us to communicate with the afterlife. You have also read about people who have seen into the future and past. And I have suggested throughout the text that people can even have glimpses of past lives. At this stage it may incongruous to believe both in reincarnation AND in a spirit world but in the next two chapters I hope to show that this is not a paradox......

You only live once..... or do you? Reincarnation is one of the world's oldest beliefs that date back to the times of the ancient Greeks and early Indian civilisations. Many people today, from all walks of life, believe that they have lived before. Here are the stories of some ordinary people with astonishing memories of lives from long ago.

Have you ever lived before? Perhaps you've had a recurring dream set in another time and place or maybe you have a nagging feeling that you were once someone else? Talk of reincarnation was once taboo but in today's tolerant times many people are coming forward to say that they are convinced that have lived before. The previous lives they describe are not necessarily about being a person of great importance. Most talk about the tedium of previous ages and often believe themselves to have been thoroughly unlikable characters.

Belief in reincarnation is common in the East, particularly among Hindus and Buddhists, but much rarer in our own culture. However the concept is not entirely alien to us. The ancient Greeks, and particularly Orpheus, Pythagoras and Plato, talk of the migration of the soul through different lives both human and animal. The early Christian Church also accepted the principle, which was expounded by Gnostics and by numerous Church fathers, including Clement of Alexandria, Origen and Saint Jerome. The doctrine was only declared a heresy 553 years after the death of Christ by the Second Council of Constantinople.

In modern times there has been a great deal of research into the claims of people who say they have remembered their previous lives. One of the best known cases concerns Shanti Devi, born in Delhi in 1926. At the age of seven she told her mother that she had been alive before, in a town called Muttra. Over the next two years her recall of events increased until she was telling her parents about her previous husband, their house, and her three children. At the age of nine a complete stranger came to the door to discuss business with her father and Shanti claimed she recognised him as her husband's cousin from her previous life.

To the astonishment of everyone the man did live in Muttra and agreed that his cousin's wife, Ludgi, had died ten years earlier. When the husband came to visit her, Shanti recognised him immediately and flung herself into his arms. When she was taken to Muttra, she was able to direct the carriage to Ludgi's house and identified her father-in-law sitting in front of it. She also recognised her two eldest children, but not the youngest, whose birth had cost Ludgi her life.

There is now a growing wealth of cases like Shanti's that are suggestive of reincarnation and today many people are exploring ways to unlock their own lost memories. Some people have spontaneous recall but there are also professional people who will help you unlock your hidden memories. Most 'Past Life Therapists' use deep relaxation sessions or hypnotic techniques to guide their client back into time. Firstly they encourage them to recall events in this life and then back into early childhood. A point comes when they can ask the subject to now look to the time before their birth and recall what they see and feel. Some describe a period between lives where they live in a heavenly afterlife but most jump straight to memories of other lives from history.

Of course this is fascinating psychological experimentation but it is also claimed that regression into past lives has a therapeutic effect. There are many cases on record to indicate that the illnesses we experience in this life are the traces left by the traumatic experiences brought forwards from past lives. For example a person suffering from severe eczema may discover that in a past life they were burnt to death. By reliving the experience they understand the root cause of their physical problems and the blemishes disappear after the therapy session. There are many cases on record where psychological problems and physical illness have been healed after a period of Past Life Therapy.

In the East reincarnation is seen as the progress of the soul through many lives on earth, as though so many grades in a school, before it 'graduates' to the immortal perfection of oneness with the infinite. Throughout this progress we accumulate *karma* which is a Sanskrit word taken from the word *Kri* to do, and is used to describe the effects of past actions. The Western equivalent would be Christ's maxim 'as ye sow so shall ye reap'. In Hinduism a man's karma follows him from incarnation to incarnation until fulfilled or spiritually transcended.

Of course all these 'memories' of past lives may be fantasy, genetic memories or even clairvoyance of the past. The brain is an incredible storehouse of unconscious memory and in hypnotic trance can be coaxed to recall vast amounts of information. A page from a book glanced at in childhood can be recalled word for word by a hypnotised adult many years later. The miraculous cures could be psychosomatic and recalling past lives may just be a way of resolving psychological problems through fantasy. The evidence for reincarnation will always be a subject for debate but the fact is that more people than ever before are coming forward to proclaim that they've lived before.

PAST LIFE MEMORIES OF MY SOUL MATE

'The other woman' in Richard King's marriage is out of this world. In fact she's never been born in the 20th century for Richard from Havant in Hampshire believes that he and his friends are in communication with his soul mate Lorelei with whom he lived many past lives. And according to Richard his wife doesn't mind. "At first she was upset that I gave my attention to someone else but gradually she's coming around. After all Lorelei is not here in the physical sense and I've obviously chosen to live this life with my wife Jo."

For 6 years Richard has been writing a 'Spiritual CV' about his past lives at the astonishing rate of 80,000 words a year. Most of this concerns the lives he's shared with his soul mate Lorelei. "My interest started in 1991 when I took part in healing workshop at the Healing Arts Festival in London" says Richard "We did some relaxation exercises and were then asked to visualise our spirit guides. At first I saw nothing, then suddenly, I saw a woman's face in full colour and vivid detail. I felt that I knew her, and that we had been deeply, physically, in love many times. It was an intense, all pervading love of such quality, depth, beauty and sheer power- beautiful beyond words and utterly devastating. It left me shattered and in tears."

It was a psychic friend, Leigh, who first referred to his new friend as Richard's soul mate. "Over the following months I came to understand the term better and realised that there was vastly more to it than the usual concept of soul mates. One Sunday evening as I sat thinking about the emotional side of my nature I heard a voice say 'That's connected with a previous life. Lorelei has already told you that.' Over the next few days an extraordinary series of coincidences, involving myself, friends and family, reinforced the connection between my soul mate and the name Lorelei.

"One evening after attending a healing session, Leigh and I were in a coffee shop. Leigh said she was seeing mountains connected with me and asked if I had been to Italy or Austria. I said that a healer had just made a similar connection.

"Then Leigh said of my soul mate Lorelei, 'She's not just anyone, she's the one to do with the legend.' Leigh asked if there was a connection somewhere with the Black Forest in Germany and the Rhine. He saw us together playing on rocks and swimming in a large river."

When Richard and Leigh searched their history books they discovered that there was a mythical woman called Lorelei. The French poet Apollinaire had written about her as goddess 'Who made all men perish from love'. According to the legends she lived near the Black Forest at the famous crag that overhangs the Rhine downstream from Bacharach in Germany.

For Richard King, Lorelei is a real personage with whom he has shared past lives. "During development circles and at other times, I began to see parts of other lives, my own and, occasionally other people's. Lives I had spent with Lorelei included one during the English Civil War. In those days she was known as Marjorie. I was called Jeremy and our children Ann-Marie and Toby."

"Some people joke that having Lorelei around is like being haunted by the ghost of an ex-wife. It is not like that. Lorelei is a powerful healing spirit. In mediumistic communications she calls my wife Jo her 'Celestial Sister'. This was proved to Jo and I when she had to have a hysterectomy. I sat in meditation asking Lorelei to send healing to her as the operation took place. I saw Jo and Lorelei surrounded in a pink cloud of healing light. The doctors were amazed at Jo's remarkable recovery and she was home within just a few days of the operation."

CASE 2: MUM TOOK ME TO THE VIETNAM WAR

Rosemary Barry (46) from Chandlers Ford, in Eastleigh, Hampshire started having waking dreams at the age of 13 and which kept recurring for 6 years. "It was like dreaming while you're wide awake" explains Rosemary "All of a sudden I would be transported back in time to Victorian times. I find myself standing by a bandstand and notice the distinctive circular patterns of the iron work. I am wearing a long dress with a small floral pattern; I have gloves on and am wearing a bonnet. At my side is a man in a military uniform. He has a sword and his tunic reminds me of the uniforms from the times of the Crimean War."

In 1970 at the age of 19 Rosemary courted a young man who we will call Michael. "Whilst in London Michael suggested that we take a walk in Richmond Park. I was overcome by an eyrie feeling of déjà vu as we walked down the paths. Although I'd never been there before I realised that I knew every detail of the place. I took Michael's hand and to his astonishment was able to show him around the park. I could tell him where the paths led and what we'd see when we turned each bend. I felt as if I was living in two worlds at the same time.

"Then the eyrie feeling got worse. My head was in a spin and I felt as if I was falling through space into an empty void. This was the place of my dreams, but now it was real. For a few moments I was standing in another time. I could see my floral dress, feel my bonnet and could see Michael beside me in full military uniform. We walked on and turned a corner. There in front of us was the bandstand with the same distinctive wrought iron work!"

Rosemary explained to Michael why she had been behaving so strangely and began to tell him of her vision. "Michael wouldn't let me finish" continues Rosemary "He confessed that he too had persistent dreams of what he believed was of a past life. He had been a soldier who had died at the 'Charge of the Light Brigade' during the Crimean War!"

Although it appears that Rosemary and Michael had shared a past life together their relationship in this life was to end. "I believe that we had to come together to resolve unfinished business" says Rosemary "We parted in sorrow at that bandstand all those years ago but were given a second chance to resolve our relationship."

The experience of recalling a past life inspired Rosemary to become a past life therapist and she now helps others recall their incarnations. She's teaches people to get into a state of light revelry similar to the waking dreams she described earlier. One of her subjects is her daughter Victoria (17). "I was quite a tomboy at the age of 13 when mum offered to take me back to my past life" explains Victoria "It was more than a phase, I loved war films and had a thing about helicopters.

"When mum guided me back I became aware that I was in Vietnam. I was an American soldier aged 21. I was a man but I was still me, it felt quite natural being male. Five of us were parachuted into the jungle but one of us was captured and we saw him executed by the Vietcong. We became angry and started shooting at the enemy even though we were greatly outnumbered. Then there was a frantic chase through the jungle as we dashed to catch the helicopters that had been sent in to pick us up. To my horror I saw one of the helicopters hit and explode. In desperation I rushed towards the second helicopter but was shot in the back and died before I could reach it."

Mum says how during her recall Victoria was crying out in anger and pain. She wept as she described events as if they were happening here and now. "There are people who may say that past life recall is a fantasy." says Rosemary. "But the subject is doing much more than story telling. They live the events and express an intensity of emotion that is totally unfamiliar to them. These impressions and feelings have to come from somewhere. I believe it is from past lives."

CASE 3 INDIANS AND COWBOYS

Ian Cugley from Deeside in Flincher was apprehensive when he decided in October last year to be hypnotised by Diane Egby-Edwards in Bournemouth. Ian is a down-to-earth man who spent much of his working life managing the staff of British Steel's stores. "I'd always felt that it's mainly sad old people looking for comfort who want to know what lies before and after this life. But I put aside my scepticism and decided to give hypnotic regression a go. To my utter surprise it answered many questions about why things are the way they are in my life."

Using hypnotism Diane was able to take Ian back to his previous life. "Although I've never travelled and I've never read history I have an uncanny ability to recall America's early history. I've never been taught it but I just *know* it." says Ian "It was this era that I found myself in when Diana took me back.

"I found myself stood looking across a very broad valley with red rock mountains in the distance. It was hot and I was being harassed by flies and I was very, very thirsty. I was wearing cavalry trousers with buck skin knee boots. I saw three ladies carrying parasols and looking at me with great suspicion.

"I walked across a street and went into a bar. As I came out I realised that I was still so very thirsty. Diana then asked me to move forward in time and I found myself on a horse travelling over some very arid land and came to some trees where there were some cavalry camped. As I approached I could sense the bad feelings coming from them. In the distance I could hear Diane's voice asking me if I'm a deserter? 'No I'm not' I replied 'I don't know what I am but they don't like me'

"I spoke to the officer in charge and complained about my thirst. I'm then brought forward by Diana and find myself walking across a plain looking for a wagon that's overdue. It's desperate that we find them. I then see that it's being chased by Indians. I say 'What am I to do?' At this point Diana tells me to look at my hands. 'Ohh' I exclaim 'I'm brown! I'm an Indian!'

"It was such a shock to me at the time and perhaps explained why nobody had given me water. I then chased after the wagon, hoping that they would realise that I wasn't hostile but I got trapped beneath it when it rolled over. Pinned beneath the wagon I experience the horror of seeing the Indians fire flaming arrows and I am burnt to death.

"The experience was so vivid, so real, that I now believe it to be memories of a past life. It also explains a lot about my own life. As a child I would be the only one in the cinema who would cheer on the Indians. Many years ago I started collecting plates portraying Indians, dream catchers and Indian mandalas and I'd always felt that the Indians are misrepresented by history. This all started way before it became fashionable to talk about Indians.

"Discovering my past life was a strange but wonderful experience. I am no longer a sceptic."

CASE 4 I FOUND MY OWN GRAVE

Jannet Stone from Birmingham added the unusual extra 'n' to her Christian name soon after her divorce. "I don't know why but I felt absolutely compelled to do it." she says "At the time I thought it was something to do with finding a new identity but I was soon to discover that the reason for my action is be found far in the past."

Jannet, like many people after a divorce, started a spiritual search to find her real self. She met hypnothereapist Rosemary Barry from Chandler's Ford in Hampshire who helped her explore her past lives by means of 'regression psychometry'. This is a psychic technique that does not involve hypnotism or trance. The psychometrist intuitively senses their clients past lives by holding an object that the person has owned for a long time and reading the 'recordings' left on it.

"I was fascinated to hear about my past lives" says Jannet "I was being told about how I once lived in Delft in Holland during the latter part of the 17th century. We were a merchant family and lived under a cloud of religious intolerance. A man was important who sailed the barges. He had given me a ring.

"Of course there was no way we could know for sure that Rosemary was getting it right. Then she looked at me and said 'I see something very important that you will be able to confirm one day. The ring has a coat of arms on it. I think it's a puffin bird, no it's a helmet seen from the side.' She then drew the picture that she was seeing. 'You'll find this in Delft, there's flowing feathers and there's a funny cross man or something above it'."

At this time Jannet was a mature student studying the history of art. "Only weeks after the consultation I was given the opportunity to go to Holland to study the paintings of Vermeer. Of course as soon as I had some free time I shot down to Delft to visit the local church and see if I could find my coat of arms."

Jannet visited St Hypolitus, Delft's old 16th century church, but was disappointed to discover that the graves had been vandalised by French invaders in 1789. All the crests and coats of arms had been hacked off. But as she turned to leave something caught her eye. "I noticed one grave by the door that had a coat of arms. My hair felt like it was curling as I saw the helmet shaped like a puffin's head, the flowing feathers and even the strange cross figure that Rosemary had tried to described. Then I looked at the inscription and nearly fell backwards. The name of one of the graves occupants spelt her name the same way as me- Jannetgen."

CASE 5: MY PAGAN LOVE AFFAIR

Amanda McCallum (32) from Gosport in Hampshire had always wanted to try hypnotic regression. When she saw hypnotist Kevin Taylor's (37) advertisement in her local newsagent's shop window she decided to give it a try. But what she uncovered was to amaze her and change her life:

"During our first session I saw myself as a male sailor in the 18th century. It was an incredible experience. I felt like a man and cursed like a man and could see scenes of 18th century Portsmouth unfolding before my eyes. I was shocked by the incredible sharpness and vividness of the experience. This was not dream or suggestion. It was as if I was really there.

"Kevin, the hypnotist, was also amazed at how easily I entered deep trance. I was such a good subject that he asked me if I would mind coming back and doing some research to see just how much we could uncover. Normally I'm so shy that I'd have said no but I liked Kevin and felt I could trust him. I agreed to help.

"Kevin and I seemed to get on with each other from the moment we met. It's quite unlike me to trust someone so implicitly but with Kevin it was as if I'd known him all my life. We continued the sessions and I remembered a number of past lives. We got on so very well that finally Kevin asked me the big question. Next time he hypnotised me could he ask me to recall if we had ever shared a past life together?

"Kevin fired the question at the next hypnotic session. I became this young woman of 18 who spoke with a tremendous self-confidence and assertiveness that was nothing like my real personality. 'I am Melissa' I heard my voice boom 'And why are you asking me such foolish questions that you know already?'

"Melissa spoke in an Old English dialect and used words such as 'hexed' which I wouldn't use in ordinary speech. When my mum listened to the tape she said that it certainly was my voice but definitely not my personality.

"Melissa told Kevin that we were in Cornwall, it was the 16th century and that she is a witch. She called Kevin, David and said that he was one of her companions. There were other companions such as a man called Simeon but he David was her favourite. David would help Melissa to gather herbs, bless babies and conduct healing rituals. I saw my past life unfold. I saw us dancing naked in water under the moonlight, ridding bareback horses along the beach and saw how David had helped me raise a child in the same way my mother had raised me to be a witch. I died at the age of 47 which I described as 'a ripe old age to die' But what amazed me most was just how different a person I was. I was cocky, authoritarian and sometimes downright vulgar.

"When I came around and woke to my normal self my cheeks flushed with embarrassment. I had only known Kevin for a month and here I was talking about dancing naked with him in the moonlight. You don't normally tell a stranger this type of thing.

"I believe that the hypnotic sessions have rekindled a romance from long ago. I'm nothing like Melissa in this life, I'm just an ordinary, down to earth mother of two. If someone had told me this same story a year ago I'd have thought them completely mad. But Kevin and I really do now believe that we lived together once before hundreds of years ago. We've talked about visiting another hypnotist to have Kevin hypnotised. I can't wait to hear what David really thought about his mentor Melissa."

CASE 6 OUR LOVE IS 3,000 YEARS OLD - AND WE CAN PROVED IT.

Josephine Sellers (51) from Millborne Port near Yeovil in Dorset recalls the day she met her future husband Brian.. "We were meant for each other and we knew it the moment our eyes met. I felt as if an electric charge shot through my body when I spotted Brian stood towering over the group of men with him. I married him at 19 and we've been together ever since.

"I believe that it was no coincidence that we met and fell in love Our coming together was predetermined because 400 years ago we had been together before. As a child I used to have memories of living in a big house and ridding in a carriage. I would ask my mother where all the people were that I once knew, the 'yesterday people' as I called them. 'And who's the vicar' I would say to my friends. Of course mother told me that this was all nonsense and in time I became as sceptical as her and about the existence of past lives. But in time my mother changed her mind.

"In the early years of our marriage we lived in London and I had a busy life working as a legal assistant. Life was so hectic that there was hardly time to think but when I stopped work and started a family something strange started to happen to me. Some mornings I would wake up and find myself in the wrong time. I'd sit up in bed and realise that I was in a luxurious Elizabethan room. I was watching events that took place hundreds of years ago. It was like watching a film except you could feel and smell everything as well. These visions would end as abruptly as they began.

"My visions triggered my interest in the paranormal and I started to meet many people who were psychic. So many of them said the same thing to me: That I'd be living in a cottage that will have a very special significance for me. This was a very odd thing to say to someone living in the London suburbs.

"One year we went to Dorset for our holidays and I just didn't want to go back home to London. I became very upset and started crying and Brian felt the same. We decided there and then that we'd close our business in London and move as soon as we could. The pull of Dorset was like a magnet.

"We finally moved and settled in a small cottage in Wimborne. The psychics' prophesies had come true.

"I felt that something had happened there in the past that I now wanted to put right. In particular I was drawn to an area called Witchampton and would go there at every opportunity."

"Brian and I started to take an interest in psychic things and after 10 years experimentation we eventually meet a trance medium named Evelyn who took no fee for her work. Spirit voices would talk directly through her. Then one day to my utter astonishment a vicar started to talk through her. 'My name is Reverend William Thomas' he said 'And I am here to tell you a remarkable tale of reincarnation.' Over a number of sessions he told us that he was the man I had seen in my childhood. He also told me how he'd had many legal battles with the crown over tenure rights. But most intriguing of all was that he said that we knew each other. I had been a woman called Catherine and had known him 400 years ago during the Elizabethan times.

"I immediately realised that I was being told things that I somehow already knew. I recorded each session and to make sure everything was authenticated correctly asked a sceptical ex-army major and ex-school master Mr John Lloyd to help research any information I was given. We continued our sessions with the medium and spoke again to the Rev William Thomas. We also made tape recordings and locked the tapes away in a bank vault. Later I met a hypnotist Diane Egby-Edwards from Bournemouth who offered to hypnotise me and take me back to my past life to see if we could retrieve any more information. An finally, I also kept careful notes of any memories that would come to me spontaneously.

"At first, I really couldn't believe what was happening. But the combined information given us from my hypnosis session, from the medium and from my own spontaneous memories gave us enough information to search the records to see if it was all true. I was told that I was named Catherine.

She was the middle daughter of five from a family of 13 children. One of my brother's names was Edmund. The vicar Rev also gave us detailed information about his legal battles with the crown

"But there was more to come. In the trance sessions the vicar told us that we had all shared this past life together. The researcher Lloyd had been the father Sir Henry who incidentally the vicar despised, and my husband had been my brother Sir Edmund. According to the vicar we had all been together in this past life 400 years ago.

"We went to the Dorset Records Office and looked to see if we could find any reverends with the name William Thomas. To our utter astonishment there was a vicar with this name for the small parish church of Chritchel later named Witchampton- the place that had obsessed me so much since we'd moved. Also we found that he was connected with a landed family called Uvedale. The father was Sir Henry Uvedale, the mother Isabell and there were thirteen children including a Catherine and Edmund. Clearly this was the family that the vicar had talked about. Also, we discovered that the vicar had, as he had told us, been my tutor and involved in a long legal dispute with the crown. Everything we had been told was true.

"We also discovered that the estate still existed although the original house had burned down. It was now owned by the Right Honourable Mary Martin who is cousin to the present Queen. We contacted her ladyship, told her our strange story and asked if we could take a look around the grounds to see if it revealed any more memories. She gave us permission and invited us for tea.

"I had remembered the big house but couldn't remember living in it. With our group was a dowser, Bob Seethon, who said he would dowse the grounds to see if there were any other buildings below the ground. He found something and suddenly the memories came flooding back. Brian and I, when we were Catherine and Edmund, hadn't lived in the big house at all. The thirteen children were such a handful that Sir Henry had build an separate nursery a quarter of a mile away from the house where we had been born. Together with the dowser we found the site.

"Afterwards we asked the Right Honourable Mary Martin if she knew if another building had stood in the grounds. Her ladyship said that her family had the original records and she believed that this was true.

"I believe that these strange events prove that Brian and I have shared a past life before. But according to the spirit of Rev William Thomas this is not our first life together. He says we also lived in the same area in 3,000 BC when I was a pagan seer who carried a jewelled wand and worshipped at the ancient standing stones.

"The evidence for our Elizabethan life together is so overwhelming that I'm prepared to take the vicar on his word."

CASE 7 THE CRIMEAN WAR SPOILED OUR ROMANCE

Rosemary Barry (46) from Chandlers Ford, in Eastleigh, Hampshire started having waking dreams at the age of 13 and which kept recurring for 6 years. "It was like dreaming while you're wide awake. All of a sudden I would be transported back in time to Victorian times. I find myself standing by a bandstand and notice the distinctive circular patterns of the iron work. I am wearing a long dress with a small floral pattern; I have gloves on and am wearing a bonnet. At my side is a man in a military uniform. He has a sword and his tunic reminds me of the uniforms from the times of the Crimean War."

"In 1970 when I was 19 I courted a young man who I will call Michael. Whilst in London Michael suggested that we take a walk in Richmond Park. I was overcome by an eyrie feeling of déjà vu as we walked down the paths. Although I'd never been there before I realised that I knew every detail of the place. I took Michael's hand and to his astonishment was able to show him around the park. I could tell him where the paths led and what we'd see when we turned each bend. I felt as if I was living in two worlds at the same time.

"Then the eyrie feeling got worse. My head was in a spin and I felt as if I was falling through space into an empty void. This was the place of my dreams, but now it was real. For a few moments I was standing in another time. I could see my floral dress, feel my bonnet and could see Michael beside me in full military uniform. We walked on and turned a corner. There in front of us was the bandstand with the same distinctive wrought iron work!

"I explained to Michael I she had been behaving so strangely and began to tell him of my vision. But Michael wouldn't let me finish. He confessed that he too had persistent dreams of what he believed was of a past life. He had been a soldier who had died at the 'Charge of the Light Brigade' during the Crimean War!"

"Although it appears that we had shared a past life together our relationship in this life was to end. I believe that we had to come together to resolve unfinished business. We parted in sorrow at that bandstand all those years ago but were given a second chance to resolve our relationship."

"The experience of recalling a past life in such detail inspired me to become a past life therapist and I now help others recall their incarnations. I teach people to get into a state of light revelry similar to the waking dreams I had myself. One of my subjects is my 17 year old daughter Victoria."

"I was quite a tomboy at the age of 13 when mum offered to take me back to my past life" explains Victoria "It was more than a phase, I loved war films and had a thing about helicopters.

"When mum guided me back I became aware that I was in Vietnam. I was an American soldier aged 21. I was a man but I was still me, it felt quite natural being male. Five of us were parachuted into the jungle but one of us was captured and we saw him executed by the Vietcong. We became angry and started shooting at the enemy even though we were greatly outnumbered. Then there was a frantic chase through the jungle as we dashed to catch the helicopters that had been sent in to pick us up. To my horror I saw one of the helicopters hit and explode. In desperation I rushed towards the second helicopter but was shot in the back and died before I could reach it."

Mum says how during her recall Victoria was crying out in anger and pain. She wept as she described events as if they were happening here and now. "There are people who may say that past life recall is a fantasy." says Rosemary. "But the subject is doing much more than story telling. They live the events and express an intensity of emotion that is totally unfamiliar to them. These impressions and feelings have to come from somewhere. I believe it is from past lives."

Are these cases that you've read suggestive of reincarnation? If so then we are presented with conflicting evidence. Either the soul goes to the afterlife or else it takes a new human birth. Which is it? I needed to know more. Perhaps the answer can be found in India.

10 MIRACLES WITH SATHYA SAI BABA

I first heard the name of Sathya Sai Baba in 1973 when I was saving the money to travel overland to India with my friend Terry. 'You must visit his ashram while you're in India' urged a fellow traveller 'Incredible things are happening there.' Unfortunately I couldn't raise the money and abandoned my yearned for trip. I never spoke or heard the name again until soon after I met Jane in 1988 when her friend Jim Chivers gave us some light grey ash (vibhutti) and suggested that we eat a little. (in chapter 1 you read about how Jim Chivers lost his son.) He told us that the ash was considered holy by the Hindus and had been materialised by the Hindu godman (Avatar) named Sai Baba.

It was soon after this that the dreams started to happen.

I had seen a photo of Sathya Sai Baba but knew nothing of his philosophy or the story of his remarkable life and miracles. The photo I saw was of a little man who wears a brilliant orange robe and has a mop of black curly hair like that of Jimi Hendrix. At the time of writing he's 72 but in the photo I saw he would have been about 45. I couldn't understand why I should start dreaming about him and why the dreams should be so remarkably vivid. These were the most amazing lucid dreams that I'd ever experienced.

My first dream was set in a garage where many cars were being fixed. Clad in his bright saffron orange robes, Sai Baba introduced himself as the chief mechanic and suggested that I come into his workshop and perhaps help a little too. He showed me how to repair car engines.

The dream made no sense.

PSYCHIC ENCOUNTERS

A few weeks later Jane and I were invited to Jim Chiver's retirement party and there we met a number of his Indian friends who were devotees of Sai Baba. I was introduced to Babu an elderly Indian man whose eyes sparkled and voice trembled when he spoke about his guru. I told him about the dream. 'It is a tremendous blessing to have a dream about Swami' he said 'Swami is calling you. He often tells his followers that he is like a mechanic of the soul and will call those that need his guidance into his workshop. When Swami comes to you in a dream it is not like a dream. It is real.'

Babu told me how a few years ago he was completely paralysed. The doctors had said that his condition was incurable and that he would remain like this for the rest of his life. He would never walk again. Babu prayed to his guru. Day and night he prayed. 'Then one night I saw an orange shimmer in my room' says Babu 'I looked again and was overjoyed to see Sai Baba appear in my room as real as you are now sat before me.'

That night the spiritual form touched Babu's feet and by the morning he could move his feet and toes. The next evening he saw Sai Baba again and the vision touched his waist. By the morning he could sit up unaided. On the third night Sai Baba touched Babu on the head and he could walk unaided. The doctors were amazed at Babu's spontaneous remission. Everyone I spoke to confirmed that he had been paralysed and had recovered. And perhaps the greatest testimony to truth was the great tears that rolled down this man's face as he told his story. I was certain that Babu was telling the truth.

Although I'd read very little about Sai Baba the dreams kept happening and Jane started having dreams too. 'I saw Sai Baba dressed in blue' Jane told me 'He asked me to sit beside him and that I was to begin spiritual healing.' He came to us both in our dreams many times and we were each shown remarkable things and given spiritual instruction that greatly helped us with our mediumistic work. I decided to find out more about Sai Baba.

Sathya Sai Baba was born in Puttaparthi, a remote village in southern India, on 23rd November 1926. His parents named the baby Sathyanarayana Raju of the Kshatriya caste. The villagers tell of signs occurring shortly before his birth such as musical instruments playing by themselves and soon after his birth a deadly cobra snake was found in his crib. Remarkably it had not harmed the baby. This event, and many others, were taken as auguries that a very special person had been born. The cobra is the symbol of *Shiva* of Hinduism's holy trinity.

At the age of 13 the young Sathya was bitten by a scorpion and after a day and night of normality fell into a coma that lasted 24 hours. When he awoke he started quoting long passages of Sanskrit poetry and philosophy that were far beyond the scope of his limited schooling. His frightened parents took him to an exorcist who shaved his head and cut three deep crosses into his skull bidding the demons to leave the child. They poured caustic material into the wounds and into his eyes. Finally, Sathya's parents could not stand to see their son suffer any more and ordered the exorcist to stop.

In May 1940 at the age of 14 the young Sathya was seen by his father materialising candy and fruit out of the air and many of the crowd that had gathered around the boy were falling to the ground and calling him an incarnation of God. His father became angry at this charade. As the father approached, ready to give the boy a beating he heard his son announce 'I am Sai Baba. My mission in this earthly sojourn shall be to lead man along the path of Dharma (righteousness) back to my feet. I have come to re-establish the Vedic way of life, to reinstate the supremacy of the spirit over matter, and to lead man back to the life of the spirit.'

He said also that he is the reincarnation of the holy man named *Sai Baba of Shirdi* who had died eight years before Sathya Sai Baba's birth. Sai Baba refers to him as 'My previous body'. None of the villagers of Puttaparthi had heard of this person but Sai Baba of Shirdi who was born a Hindu but lived with a Moslem family. On his head he wore a piece of cloth called a Kani. Like today's Sai Baba he could perform miracles and before his death had predicted where and when he would be reborn in eight years time. These details corresponded exactly to the time and place of Sai Baba's birth as recorded by Kaka Dikshit in 1918. Many of Sai Baba's first devotes were followers of Sai Baba of Shirdi. Sai Baba was even able to prove his spiritual lineage by recounting events and the details of private conversations spoken during his previous incarnation. He tells us that he will need a third incarnation to complete his work as Prema Sai. He claims to be an Avatar which broadly means the descent of the Divine principle into the human state. In other words Sai Baba is the formless God taking form.

If Sai Baba's claim is true the implication is that he is not just tapping into the source of knowledge but that he is all knowledge. "My power is immeasurable, my truth inexplicable, unfathomable, I am beyond the reach of the most intensive enquiry and the most meticulous measurement. There is nothing I do not see, nowhere I do not know the way, no problem I cannot solve My sufficiency is unconditional. I AM the Totality. All of it."

My reaction to statements such as this was that it is a preposterous proposal. How can an infinite God take form? For example, it has always irritated me how Christians say that you can't believe in God unless you also believe in Jesus Christ. 'Then give me Hell with the company of Socrates, Gandhi and Loa Tzu' I love to tell these blinkered believers. God is an infinite state that exists both within us and without us, people such as Jesus, Buddha, Mohammed and so on are, in the words of a Zen poet, 'the finger that points at the moon but not the moon itself.' Nobody I believed should stand in the way of direct experience of God- not even Jesus or Sai Baba.

A few months after Sai Baba's declaration a group of villagers pleaded with him that he show them a sign to confirm that he is who he claims to be. To the surprise of all assembled he immediately threw a bunch of jasmine flowers onto the ground. In the local Telugu script the petals clearly spelt out the words 'Sai Baba'.

Miracles such as these have been happening, and still happen, around Sai Baba ever since he began his mission. He says that they are there to prove to his devotees that he is who he says he is. He calls them his 'visiting cards'. He manifests material objects, sacred ash (vibhuti), has changed an object from one object to another simply by blowing on it and many, many more instances and before thousands of people. 'They are neither magical tricks nor Siddhic powers.' says Sai Baba 'These can come to everybody with the appropriate discipline and yoga exercises, but my powers to protect, heal and save people and materialise objects originate in God, and can be used only by an Avatar. They are in no way designed, disciplined or developed, but flow from Cosmic Power itself.'

At the same interview he was also asked if his powers come from the spirit world who in the past have manifested apports and materialisations through mediums and yogis. "There is no need for me to command invisible spirits since my own divine will materialises the objects. I am everything, everywhere, omniscient, omnipotent and omnipresent; and so whatever I will instantly happens. Like the qualities of truth, love and peace, these are things that generate the Atmic or Cosmic forces behind the Universe." As a child he had announced that till the age of 16 he will be mostly engaged in sportive pursuits, and that from then on until the age of 32, he will be drawing people to him by means of Mahimas or miracles. He says that without this display of power 'no one can gauge even a fraction of my glory.'

Many well respected authors have investigated the miracles of Sathya Sai Baba for decades. There is not enough space here to cover their stories and

I do not want to repeat information that you can read elsewhere in detail. If you'd like to find out a little more I suggest you read any of the books by the following authors: Howard Murphet, Dr John Hislop, Dr Samuel Sandweiss or the catholic priest Don Mario Mazzoleni.

Some of the reports that you will read about Sai Baba's miracles are mind boggling. He has supposedly raised the dead, multiplied food as Christ did with the bread and fishes, materialised valuable objects out of the air and turned water into petrol when the car ran out of fuel. There are stories of him materialising sweets directly into people's mouths, appearing in two or more places at the same time and projecting a photograph of Christ onto the film in someone's camera. His devotees have witnessed paranormal and psychic phenomena for which no common-sense explanation is possible. With a wave of his hand he can materialise sweets, images, idols, flowers, fruits, rosaries and crucifixes. So numerous, so well attested and so extraordinary are these accounts that even the most die-hard sceptics find these 'miracles' hard to explain away.

Jane and I kept having the dreams about Sai Baba. Eventually I felt compelled to write about him in my books and newspaper columns. I mentioned him in *The Scottish Daily Record, The Weekly News, The Portsmouth News* and Bristol's *Western Daily Press*. In addition I posted one of the articles on my Internet website (http://psychics.co.uk) and started to receive some very interesting telephone calls and letters.

I did not consider myself a devotee but nonetheless had a great respect for the wisdom his teachings. He claims to be omnipresent so if this really is the case, I argued to myself, then he would be able to give me an answer as to whether I should write the article.

I closed my eyes and randomly opened a pile of papers about him that had been given me to me by a friend Johnny Diamond who had downloaded and printed them from off the Internet. I struck the page with a pin and read part of a quote of his 'It is time the world knew'. I picked up the phone to interview Joan Brake from Porishead in Somerset who had written to my column. "It's all right to talk about Sai Baba now you know" said Joan " He says 'It is time the world knew'."

So with the hairs standing on the back of my neck I began the interview with this lovely spiritual lady. Joan and her husband Richard first heard about the miracles and teaching of Sai Baba over eleven years ago. Their search for spiritual truth began within Spiritualism and says Joan "we found that without a shadow of a doubt that life goes on after death".

Joan and Richard's search continued and they researched healing, clairvoyance, meditation, reflexology, crystal therapy and Native American teachings. "If anything came along with a spiritual aspect, Richard and I would look into it and share what we found with others" Inevitably perhaps, Joan and Richard opened their home and once a month invited experts and lecturers to talk to her growing group. "One by one they started to talk about Sai Baba- even though it was not the subject they'd come to talk about"

"I listened to the talks and saw videos of Sai Baba performing miracles and although it was plain that he was a wonderful man, he was not doing or saying anything different to what Christ said and after all magicians like Paul Daniels can perform similar 'miracles' on television. This type of thing has to be real for me. I can't accept everything people say is true"

But Richard and Joan became more and more intrigued. "The people who spoke or wrote about Sai Baba weren't 'wild' or 'hippie' types they were professional people such as doctors so we decided that if Christ was alive today then I'd want to go and see him. And if, from what I'd read and heard, Sai Baba was doing the same things as Christ then we would have to go and find out for ourselves."

Joan and Richard Brake joined a party of 90 people who had made the same decision and flew to India. Nowadays Sai Baba is surrounded by so many followers that it is almost impossible to get near him. On his 70th birthday (Nov 23rd) he had over one million visitors to his ashram (Spiritual Centre) yet every one of them was housed and fully fed for free. Joan and Richard were lucky. They were invited to meet Sai Baba for a private audience with him.

"Years and years ago there was a song in the hit parade called 'Open the door Richard'" says Joan "A family joke, that continued for years, was to change the words and sing 'Close the door Richard' every time Richard entered a room. Richard was the last to enter Sai Baba's private chambers. With a twinkle in his eye Sai Baba looked at him and in the correct tune actually sang the words 'Close the door.....Richard'! Sai Baba then turned round , looked at me, and roared with laughter.

"Nobody else in that room knew what was going on but for Richard and I it was incredible that Sai Baba should know this little family joke from so long ago. It was absolutely fantastic."

Joan and Richard have since had a number of private interviews with Sai Baba over the years. "On many occasions we've seen him materialise objects from thin air" continues Joan "On one occasion he materialised a silver medallion with his image imprinted on it which was passed round. He then blew on it and it changed into a little golden statue of the Hindu elephant god Ganesha with three rubies hanging from it. This again was passed around. Sai Baba then looked at one of the visitors and said 'What do you want?' 'You Swami was the reply' so Sai Baba blew on it again and back came the medallion."

"I've seen him materialise rings with pictures of Christ on them, vibhuti ash, silver boxes.. a whole list of things." But Joan stresses that the phenomena Sai Baba displays are unimportant. "When he looks at you know that he knows everything about you. I cannot explain the feeling of overwhelming love you feel in his presence. It's not hysterical, it's a silent, inward transformation."

So what is the message that this Eastern teacher can give to the West? "His teachings are simply profound" answers Joan "Everyone can identify with what he says. It's like he's brought all the ancient wisdom up to date. Yet he's not trying to convert people or make them change their faith. A Christian should remain a Christian a Hindu a Hindu etc. Perhaps it can best be expressed by quoting his words: 'There's only one religion- the religion of love. There's only one language- the language of the heart. There's only one cast- the cast of humanity. And there's only one God- and he is omnipresent."

I also received a number of interesting emails to my web site. This one from a doctor was very interesting:

'About myself: I'm a medical doctor 43 years old with about 20 years experience and now in a private practice. I came to know about Sathya Sai Baba of Puttaparthi, India about 3 years ago, and ever since have got stuck to Him. It is beyond my comprehension to explain his miracles. I write to you with my first hand experiences, to tell you about something that I've observed with my own eyes: One day I noticed liquid coming out the picture of Sai Baba from outside the glass. It was pouring out from the site of his blessing palm, but only little in quantity. It dripped down slowly. My wife is also medical doctor. I've 2 daughters, one 7 years, one 9 years. There's no foul play. The question is: How can this liquid issue forth from the picture of Sai Baba, from the glass outside? In fact the neighbouring Lord Ganesha picture was 'sweating' similar amrith also from all over the glass. (Amrith is a sweet necture that tastes like honey.) How on earth can we explain this, that is the question. Since you expound the unexplainable, please explain this phenomena.'

The doctor had witnessed a phenomena that has been occurring in many homes throughout the world where vibhutti and its liquid equivalent amrith materialises on photographs of Sai Baba.

Jane our daughter Danielle (8) and were to experience this first hand. One of my readers telephoned me and asked if I'd like to visit a house in London where vibhutti ash was materialising all the time. I was told that it regularly appeared on photographs of Sai Baba. He could make an appointment for us to visit and witness this for ourselves.

The little house in Kingsbury, London was nothing special to look at. It was a typical suburban house set in a non-descript area of the capital near Neasden. It would have been hard to deliberately choose a more unremarkable setting for a miracle to happen.

We were greeted by Bhasker Joshi and his wife Hema who welcomed us into their home and lead us into their living room. The whole house was filled with the subtle jasmine scented perfume of the vibhutti ash which covered the many photographs that hung around the room. For a few moments we stood in silence looking at the surreal scene. 'The writing, which is a little hard to read under the ash, says "Love Swami", it appeared by itself and the cross of vibhutti on this picture appeared on Good Friday.' said Basker 'The photos were completely covered but we removed the area around Swami's face. If we clear a section of the pictures the vibhutti reforms.'

I was reminded of Sai Baba's words: 'My shakti, my power, my mystery can never be understood, whosoever may try, for however long a period, by whatever means.' Once we had time to absorb the wonderful atmosphere of this place we sat down with Mr & Mrs Joshi and they told us their remarkable story:

'I am of Bramin caste so was brought up in the ways of the Hindu religion' began Basker, 'but nothing prepared my for the marvellous experiences I was to have on discovering Sai Baba when I was in Uganda in 1968. This was the only time Swami has left India but I sat with about 2,000 people to get sight of him. This is called Darshan which means 'sight of the divine'. Sai Baba points his finger at me. "Go inside" my friend Dr Patel urges me. "He wants to see you in the interview room!"

' Once I entered the room I touched Swami's feet as is Hindu custom. Sai Baba smiled at me the waved his hand and materialised a photograph of himself.' Mr Basker passed round the crumpled black and white photograph. 'I have a knack of loosing things but this photograph has been upon my person every day since the interview. He knew everything about my life and told me how to resolve many personal problems which no-one except myself and God knew about. To my wife Hema he turned and said "I am in this house"

"In 1994 at Sai Baba's 69th birthday celebrations in Harrow, London we met Stephen Turoff who is a famous trance healer and now a Sai Baba devotee. He glassy entranced eyes looked at Hema "I will see you tonight" he said. But it wasn't Stephen's voice, we all distinctly heard the soft tones of Baba.'

Hema excitedly takes up the story: 'The next night I awoke in the middle of the night and see Sai Baba stood in our bedroom! He walked towards me and I felt him touch my forehead. "Your problems are over I am in your house now" he said then disappeared. In the morning we discovered that vibhutti had materialised in the prayer room, on the pictures of our Hindu deities and on photographs of Sai Baba.'

'The phenomena have continued ever since' says Basker 'And we are not the only people to experience this phenomena in our home. 'Nearby at Queensbury Mr Vadagama has been having vibbhuti materialise in the machines at his factory. He tells us that one day he had an 8 ton machine to move over a bank holiday but was let down at the last minute. If the machine wasn't moved immediately he would loose a great deal of money as the tenant was to move in the next day. Like a good Hindu he prayed in his heart for help.

'A slim man in oily jeans walked into the warehouse. He had a lorry parked outside. "You want to move the machine?" he said nonchalantly. Mr Vadagama asked the man if he could help and how much would it cost. He gave the man £75 which he counted slowly with his oily hands. Mr Vadagama turned his back for a few seconds to discover that the man had gone and to his utter bafflement saw that the eight ton machine was all neatly dismantled and stacked on the truck.

'Two years later Mr Vadagama went to Puttaparthi and was seated among other devotees for Darshan. Sai Baba walked up to him. "Is your machine all right?" asked swami with a broad smile across his face. "You gave me £75 didn't you? I put it back in the machine go and check" Immediately afterwards Mr Vadagama telephoned his daughter who was minding the business back in London. He told him where Sai Baba had said the money was and his daughter went to check. "It's all there and has oily finger prints all over it." came the excited reply '.

As far as I can tell Mr and Mrs Joshi are sincere people. They went on to tell me how the vibhutti ash will fill various sweet jars in the room upstairs that is set up as Baba's own room. Also how amrith will pour from the pictures at auspicious times, even food that is put before their temple is eaten. My credibility was beginning to strain. It could of course all be a well meant hoax. Inwardly I asked Sai Baba for a tangible sign to prove that this was all true. Moments later a lady who had arrived at the same time as us opened the prayer letter that she had placed on the alter- to her astonishment the pages inside were covered in a light sprinkling of vibhutti ash.

I also had an interesting email correspondence with Bon Giovanni an Italian who has a website dedicated to Sai Baba. He spotted my articles on my website and wrote to me to correct a few names that I had misspelled. As Bon Giovanni had clearly had personal experience of Sai Baba's miracles I asked him to clear up a problem I had: Reading the many books about Swami, I'd noticed that Sai Baba had contradicted himself. For example to one devotee he said that spiritual healing was good and to another that it was bad. He has also been asked if there is life on other planets and if there are really UFOs. Again he appears to offer us a contradiction.

Here's a small part of the explanation offered by Don Giovanni:

'Swami had taken a group of students and two elders out to a forest reserve, wild animals you know, and all had sat down for tiffen, seated in a horseshoe around Baba at the centre of the group. A student keen on such things then asked Swami why he had told differing accounts to people about UFO's, since he really wanted to know if they were or were not real. Swami looked at the young man and started to answer, but at that moment in the field behind him, in broad daylight, a UFO appeared and just hovered there in the sky above the group. Not even looking back behind him, Baba calmly said `UFO's are just imagination', and the craft vanished.

'Since that is important for you, as you say, then perhaps as you find `contradictions' in what Swami says, I suggest you examine very, very, very carefully why it bothers you, and see what happens. "Could be." I truly no longer harbour such thoughts, and so cannot answer you. You see, Swami does extraordinary things. Sometimes he does such miracles that the mind simply caves in, and at other times he does such clumsy sleight of hand tricks you think that he must think you are a fool if he expects you to fall for it. Why does he do that? Why does he contradict himself? Why is he so damnably indefinable? My hunch is that he does whatever is appropriate to further the insight of the individual present before him, no matter if that somehow makes the person think of him as a fraud or a god. He really does not care what one thinks of him, you see. At least that is my experience. Just when I think I have Swami pegged, he does something outside my comprehension. When doubt overwhelms me, I later discover why I have learned just as much from that process as when wisdom overwhelms me.

'No doubt you are wondering what I mean about palming objects. Swami is seated in private with four or five of us, and opens his empty right hand, palm up. He says, `see it is coming' and in a few seconds, just ABOVE his palm, a golden ring appears in mid-air, then falls into his hand. He passes it around. The metal is warm to the touch. Swami tells a story about how changing the heart of man into gold is not his job, but ours, and it takes effort, heat. At that moment a student enters to deliver a message. Swami then very clumsily palms the very ring he had just materialised and we all see him palming it, but he then waves his hand as if creating an object, and no surprise "produces" the gold ring, which he gives the student. I could almost feel the student's thoughts "but but but you palmed that!" .We all knew the student had not seen it appear in mid-air, and I for one thought surely the boy was now filled with doubts about Swami. `Why he just palms things!

'Why does he do such things? FIND OUT! Sorry to be so Zen, but that is my experience: one must find out for oneself. After you have seen him and come to know him directly, perhaps your questions about contradictions will be satisfied.'

Bon Giovanni had put his finger on something that I was beginning to understand. The experience of Sai Baba is unique to every individual. Many people may witness a miracle but it will mean something completely different to everyone who witnesses it. The reality of Sai Baba's miracles was hammered home to me soon after the email during a series of psychic consultations I was doing at someone's home in Portsmouth.

A somewhat burly gentleman sat down for his reading and, to my surprise, I noticed that he was wearing a platinum bracelet with an Indian Om symbol on it. It seemed completely out of place on such a big man who I found out later was a builder. I asked him if the bracelet was from Sai Baba and he told me his wonderful story. ' I burst into tears when Sai Baba materialised the bracelet for me. He was as close to me as you are now" he said "There was no way it could have been fraud. Swami pointed upward with his finger and I could see a circle of sparkling light swirling above it. Then, to my utter astonishment, I saw the circle of light form into this bracelet hovering in the air six inches above his index finger. Sai Baba then opened his hand and the bracelet dropped into it."

Again, I couldn't help but notice that this big man had tears in the corner of his eyes as he spoke.

My favourite person who sent me his stories was Bhupendra Desai a retired school master who now runs a newsagent's shop in Birmingham and spends all of his spare time painting pictures of Sai Baba. His voice quivers with joy as he tells his story:

'In my opinion Sai Baba's greatest miracle is his ability to cause transformation in our hearts and to awaken our natural divinity.' writes Desai in his first letter 'I went to India this year to see Sai Baba with a group of followers. On 20th January I saw him materialise a gold and diamond watch for a young devotee. He then took another devotee's steel ring from his finger and blew on it. We saw it change into a diamond ring. Baba recently also materialised a small Bible containing facts about Jesus. Tears of joy flooded my eyes to see such wonders.

'Later I witnessed another marvel. I saw a statue of Sai Baba- as his first incarnation as Shirdi Baba- drink milk from a little pot which was offered by the Hindu priest. In India this is called the abhishekam ceremony and your readers may remember how this hit the headlines sometime ago when statues, even brass statues, from all over the world started drinking milk. These miracles are interpreted as proof that the formless God can also take form.

'The statue of Baba that I saw drinking milk was five feet high and made of solid marble. There was no hollow for the mouth. As it drank the milk I could hear it slurp. It drank half a pot every day.

'Recently I was talking to John, a customer at my newspaper shop, about the miracles of Sai Baba and I felt so sorry for him that gave the man some of vibhuti ash. Sometime ago he had damaged his neck and the doctors said that there was nothing more they could do for him. He had over the years visited many specialists and private doctors.

'I gave him four packets of vibhuti and a photograph of Sai Baba. The vibhuti I gave him had been given to me by Dr D Gadhia who is a very old devotee who has been helping teach Baba's teachings about love, truth, right conduct, non-violence and peace. This vibhuti was in fact extracted from his own body coming out of his hands and from his legs particularly at night. This phenomena lasted for three months and everyday devotees from all over the UK were going to his home in Leicester to see him and would see vibhuti everywhere- even in his bed sheets.

'I told him to keep these packets under his pillow and under his bed sheet. I also told him to pray to his own chosen God incarnation. I believe he prayed to the Lord Jesus Christ.

'John also told me how during the healing process the photo of Sai Baba would move from room to room yet there were no children or pets in the house that could of done this when his back was turned. This is just one example of healing that Baba can do.
Within a week John could turn his neck 45 degrees. I two weeks he was fully cured and could hold his head straight and without any pain. He returned to my shop to thank me "It has nothing to do with me" I said "It is Baba who has blessed you."

Bhupendra Desai sent me many more incredible stories which I'm afraid will have to wait for another book. His 'Sai Stories' and the many others that I was told were intriguing me more and more. Devotees seemed to be crawling out of the woodwork to tell me their stories. And the dreams kept happening. My aunt Marion, my father, my sister and even our daughter Danielle dreamed of Sai Baba. I couldn't put it off any longer, I had to go to India to see for myself.

But it was more than curiosity that was calling me. The Spiritualist side of me could quite easily accept the phenomena of materialisation which had already been proved many times in the seance rooms. More importantly, Sai Baba had somehow connected with me on a very deep level of my being. I was still aware of the spirit world and of my guiding spirits but now there was another voice within me, a voice that even the angels bowed down too. I was beginning to believe that Sai Baba really was what he claimed. He is omnipresent.

So why go to India? I considered my reasons and motives carefully and once I'd siphoned off all the junk there remained two key issues that I felt I should address. Firstly the journey would be spiritually good for Jane and myself and we'd find out once and for all if Sai Baba is really what he says he is. Furthermore a pilgrimage to India would help us to progress spiritually and hopefully turn us into better people with a clearer understanding of the purpose of life. Finally, I needed to know what Sai Baba had to say about the work that people like Jane and myself do. Is it right to communicate with the Afterlife? How best should we use our psychic powers? And does reincarnation entail the survival of the individuality? As a Spiritualist I have always believed that the whole human personality including its memories and character survives bodily death. Perhaps Sai Baba could help to unify the many aspects of my work which you have read about here. I made a few phone calls and booked to join a small group of four female devotees who would be travelling to the ashram in early November.

I will never forget the look of horror on Jane's face as we walked through the airport in Bangalore. Even the swarms of mosquitoes that feasted on our pink flesh appeared to have to fight their way through passport control and then only to have countless forms signed and stamped in triplicate by illiterate clerks. Fortunately I found a trolley that wasn't being slept on and we forced our way to the pre-booked taxi as God knows how many 'porters' grabbed our luggage. A crowd of 'volunteers' also helped bump-start the rusting Morris Oxford with one hand twisted awkwardly through the broken window. 'Tip Auntie! Auntie, Auntie tip!' we could hear the voices outside call to Jane. The cab coughed black smoke and leapt into life as if relieved to escape from the clamouring crowd and once again bounce its way down the pot-holed streets like a uncontrolled kango hammer. Brakes, steering, suspension and windscreen wipers are considered optional accessories in the Bangalore taxi services.

We spent the night in a hotel that was as exquisite as my garage and owned by a doppelganger of Mr Bean. (He even picked his nose in the same way) After an extensive shopping trip around the run down shoe shops of Bangalore with my five women companions now satiated by shopping we boarded the taxi again and headed off into the wilds of the countryside. As we passed a sneering statue of Queen Victoria still overseeing her 'garden city' I felt a little guilty at pressurising Jane to make this journey. But she entered the spirit of things and her day to day worries about new carpets, decorating and DIY now seemed so far away. More immediate was the need to know whether we would survive the taxi journey as our scrap car belted at full throttle down the rugged roads to the village of Puttaparthi or if out luggage would stay on the roof rack. As the car swerved to avoid children, squeezed between juggernauts and sped at oncoming traffic I learnt the spiritual lesson of how to pray with all my heart.

'We're all likely to go through a cleansing process on arrival' said Carol Alderman our experienced group leader 'It tends to happen to most people at first. Don't ask me why, but you may experience some negative feelings.'

I certainly didn't anticipate any problems between anyone in our little group. Jane and I were in good spirits, Carol was a bit bossy but also a good organiser, Pria was a trainee doctor and radiated compassion, Linda was very easy going and Annie a textile designer was helpful and cheery. We were a smashing crowd. And of course I was so spiritually advanced that I wouldn't encounter any problems. So what could Carol possibly mean by saying this?

Even though we were all nearly dropping dead with jet lag and tiredness Carol urged us to quickly clean and tidy our rooms so that we could catch the afternoon *Darshan*. This is held in the mandir which is a magnificent open sided temple with wonderful pink, blue and yellow carvings intertwined in its pillars, domes and structure. Darshan is a Sanskrit word that means 'The sight of a holy being' and translates literally as: 'to breath the same air as'. According to the Hindus, just to have sight of a personage with the spiritual magnitude of Sai Baba brings tremendous blessing and triggers a spiritual transformation within the beholder. I was soon to find out what this meant.

As I sat in the lines waiting to be lead into the Mandir to view Sai Baba I listened to the crows squawking overhead and though about the dream that I had just prior to leaving England. I'd dreamed of arriving at the *Prasanthi Nilayam* ashram by coach and of being immediately called in to see Sai Baba for a private consultation. Was this wishful fulfilment or was I going to be called here and now?

The *Darsha* lines are called by drawing lots. I was sat close to the front of one row and my row was called first. I was led by Sai Baba's volunteers (*Sevadals*) to the very front of the area where Sai Baba would walk. we sat for about an hour as everyone else was crammed into the huge building. Then a great hush fell over the crowd and even the birds and monkeys stopped chattering as a small orange form appeared at the far side of the Mandir where the rest of my group and the other women sat. I could see Sai Baba floating like an orange flower on a sea of silence. Things were happening inside my head that I couldn't begin to explain. All my life I had spoken out against gurus yet here I was sat basking in awe at this person.

There were even tears in my eyes. So this is what they meant by *Darshan*.

Throughout my life I have been able to clearly see the human aura. As I looked at the little figure in the distance I could see great waves of light pouring from him in every colour imaginable. He seemed to be showering us with light and everyone present could feel it. I saw him speak to a few women on the other side who got up and walked to behind the pillars near the entrance to the inner sanctuary. Other people got up when told to but I couldn't see if Jane or our group had been called.

Eventually he walked to the area where I was sitting on the floor. He was stood right in front of me and materialised vibhutti ash from his fingers and into the hands of devotees nearby. I was so close that could see exactly what was happening just in front of me. The ash was appearing a few inches away from his fingers. 'My God this is really happening!' Then something happened inside me that is impossible to explain. It was as if something cracked. I could even hear it snap like a silent explosion within. I felt overwhelmed.

Sai Baba walked on stopping now and again to talk to others then finally completing his circuit and joining the people who had gathered behind the pillar. The instant he was out of sight most of the crowd rose to their feet and thronged towards the exits. As I turned to leave one of the Sevadals came up to me and touched my scarf that Carol had given to me to mark out our group. All around there were people wearing scarves from every country of the world. Apparently if one member of a group is called in to see Sai Baba then all the rest can follow.

'UK? UK?' said the sevadal urgently. 'Yes UK' I replied puzzled why he should single me out. 'Your group has been called. Quickly, quickly follow me Swami will see you but you must hurry.' I don't think my heart has ever pounded so hard. Now at last I could ask all my questions. And goodness knows what else will happen. Another sevadal joined him and I was rushed towards the front. 'No, No. Too late. Sorry you miss Swami. Very sorry.'

I walked slowly away from the Mandir and into the strange unfamiliar world of the ashram.

This was the story of my life. My biggest grudge is that so often I've come inches away from success then had the prize whisked away from me at the last minute. There are points in my life when I was nearly a famous artist, nearly a rich man, nearly had my own TV show with Jane, nearly met Sai Baba in person. In addition I thought about how so many times people had greatly profited by plagiarising my ideas or have stolen my opportunities by jumping on contacts that had worked hard to establish.

On the ashram time appears to stand still yet also seems so limited. It felt like an eternity that I wandered the ashram grounds contemplating the significance of what had happened. Yet in that short period time I resolved a major inner barrier to my personal happiness. In my Spiritualist work as a medium I had always talked about service and Sai Baba is quoted as saying that we should 'give up the fruits of our actions'. So what if I didn't get the rewards that I believed I deserved. These things are in God's hands. The important thing is that I do my spiritual work and all work in the spirit of service and without thought of reward. Any benefits are just the footprints left in the changing sands of time.

Carol was right about the cleansing process we'd go through. Once I'd resolved my inner test I started to feel relief and a growing pleasure with the thought that Jane and the girls had had an interview and I felt eager to know what wonderful things had happened. 'How did it go?' I asked once I'd found them. 'Oh fine' said Pria as if it was something that happened every day. 'The interview, what happened in the interview?' I continued. They all looked at me puzzled 'What interview?' they said almost in unison.

It transpired that there were two UK groups at the ashram and we had identical scarves.

Most people who go to see Sai Baba say that it's the inner transformation that is more remarkable that any physical miracles that Sai Baba performs. Sai Baba gives each visitor an 'inner view' and just like the spirit guides that can communicate to us through our mind so too does the powers of Sai Baba extend into this other dimension of existence. These 'inner views' can take place anywhere without having to keep visiting the ashram. I consequently realised also that a personal interview was perhaps unnecessary. What happens in the ashram is a uniquely personal experience and completely subjective yet relevant to the individual. Everybody who goes discovers something completely different.

Our group leader Carol Alderman had other ideas. From the moment we left she was desperate for a personal interview. This was quite understandable because the last time she had come she was instructed by

Sai Baba to write a course for the Sathya Sai Education in Human Values Organisation. EVH as it is called is now an intricate part of the Indian Education system and has been introduced into schools throughout the world. The programme has a multi-cultural and multi-faith approach. The system teaches that at the core of all religions lie the same fundamental values by which we should govern our lives. These are right conduct, peace, truth, love and non-violence which are fundamental in the make-up of the human personality.

Before we'd left Carol let me have a look at part of the vast amount of work she had done. On an earlier visit to the ashram two years before in 1966 Sai Baba had called her to an interview to approve the first stage. 'When he had finished looking through the books he said "Very happy. Very happy. Good girl."' says Carol, ' During the interview he also turned to me and said "Where did you get that necklace?"

"You gave it to me, swami," I replied.

"Yes," he smiled. "I gave it to you last time."

'The gold necklace he was teasing me about was one he had materialised in an interview in November 1995. I had shown him the first book I had written from which the current books have been born. He had asked if I would promote the Programme in the UK and I had thought, "But it will be difficult. I will need your help, Swami" Before the thought had even finished, he had waved his hand and produced a necklace of 101 golden beads with little symbols on them. He then put it over my head and told me never to take it off. And I never have. It is a constant reminder of his presence day and night, reminding me, amongst other things, that he is the doer and I am merely the instrument. I have had so much evidence of this over the last two years that I know I have nothing to worry about or plan. It all happens as he wills.'

Many famous people have visited Sai Baba and come away from the experience feeling that they were not in the presence of an ordinary human being. For example Sarah Fergison, the Duchess of York, visited the ashram and met Sai Baba on 30th January 1997. Although sneered at by the press as a 'Madam Vasso experience in a spiritual Disneyland' I discovered that Fergie had a deeply moving spiritual experience. She was granted a private interview and asked Sai Baba to materialise her a cross and chain. Without hesitation Sai Baba waved his hand and materialised exactly what she asked for. Apparently Fergie was deeply shaken and spiritually inspired by the encounter. Others that have been include Rolf Harris, who has given lectures at the ashram, Michael Jackson and Hillary Clinton who secretly made a visit. It was rumoured that Princess Diana had visited Sai Baba while she was at Bangalore. She sent out a report to the press saying that she wouldn't be attending her functions due to a throat infection. During this time she sneaked into the ashram.

Shortly after our journey to the ashram Sarah Miles, the daughter of actor Sir John Miles, visited the ashram for Christmas. 'Although I never got near him all the time I was in Puttaparthi, I received many real Christmas presents from Sai Baba, none of them costing a penny and all of them changing my life.

'Sai Baba is not well served by talk - experiencing him is all. And while I may never go to Puttaparthi again, nor ever understand where the love comes from out there, I do know that that love is truly blinding. How blesses those temple birds are, to be forever surrounded by it.'

We too never received a personal interview but I realised that this was not important. It's what happens inside you that counts. Nonetheless we met many people whose lives had been changed, people who'd been healed and others who had been graced with materialised objects and jewellery. Carol Alderman stayed on for a couple of months after we left. I dare not think how desperate she was by this time for an interview. She'd been urging us to take on all sorts of austerities in order to win Sai Baba's favour. It didn't work. 'Perhaps we should all wear stones in our shoes?' I joked. For a brief moment her face betrayed that she was taking me seriously. After we left Carol's husband joined her.

Then at the very last Darshan before Carol had to leave for her flight Sai Baba said to her husband. 'Husband interview? Oh yes husband interview. Of course husband interview.' Carol of course could join him.

Sai Baba kept 'accidentally' treading on her toes and spent most of the interview giving all his attention to her husband Bob. Sai Baba showed his approval of the books by stoking them fondly as he spoke to Bob. Right up to the last minute Sai Baba was playing his game. Of course he knew how desperate Carol was for an interview. He'd known this all along. Finally he turned to Carol as she went to go. 'Now you open a school in the UK'. The huge task that Sai Baba nonchalantly requested is gradually taking shape- but that's another amazing story.

They say that nobody goes away from the presence of Sai Baba disappointed. I certainly felt inspired and uplifted by the experience and many, many questions had been answered. But as our time to leave approached I felt a little sad that I hadn't been able to ask Sai Baba directly about the afterlife and the survival of the human personality after death. Just before we left a man who I'd not seen before made a casual remark. 'The answer to your questions about the afterlife are to be found in the books by Peggy Mason' said the stranger 'She has the answer'. I of course wondered how he had known my question and we were separated by the crowd before I could ask him.

When we returned to home we were greeted by our usual mountain of letters. Amongst them was a package from Peggy Mason.

I'd read one of her book in the past and posted a letter to her sometime ago but nonetheless it seemed very odd that I should arrive so perfectly on cue. She enclosed all the information she had about Sai Baba and the afterlife. "Of course reincarnation entails the survival of the individuality' writes Peggy "One of my favourite quotes of Baba's: "The good fortune that has brought you face to face with me is something for which you must thank your merit won through previous lives."

'Baba knew, of course, that for many years my late husband (Ron Lang) and I had the most gifted medium living in our staff cottage when we had a big place near Crowborough. For 14 years I wrote monthly articles for the Spiritualist magazine 'Two Worlds' when Maurice Barbanell was editor. As many people are so ignorant about mediumship and the continuation of the individual after leaving the physical body, we made a point of asking Baba, in private interview, for the sake of other people "Is mediumship, to communicate with those in the next sphere of life, provided the medium is honest and a pure channel wrong?'

'Baba replied at once: "No, not at all."'

Peggy Mason included a wealth of material, none of which conflicts with what I've tried to communicate through this book. The full details will have to wait for another book. Peggy went on to explain that she was still in touch with her husband via an excellent trance medium (Paul Bura) concludes by saying: 'My husband Ron is of course longing for me to join him! He has it all prepared, and has a lovely little house by a lake, and our beloved sheepdog Tippy with him, and my cat Peter (And adds: "And you don't have to feed them!) He works with a group of spirits helping those who go over "without a clue, wondering what on earth has happened to them"' as he puts it.

'When I asked him what it was like to be received by Baba when he passed over, he said "Like being embraced by the Universe". He also says he and Baba will come for me. My health is running down, plus angina etc. so I don't expect to be here beyond next Summer....'

A few weeks later I read in *Psychic News* that Peggy Mason had died.

11 ARE YOU PSYCHIC? FAQ

According to a MORI survey made in 1998 more than nine out of ten people - an astonishing 92 per cent of the population - believe in the paranormal yet only 64 per cent believe in God. The pollsters also discovered that four out of ten believe in ghosts and one in seven claim to have been spooked by one. Six in ten believe in premonitions, 30 per cent are convinced dreams can tell the future and 54 per cent say telepathy works. Over half of the UK population have experienced déjà vu. Also, just over ten percent have been to a fortune teller, the same number who have been to a medium. Eight per cent say the future has been predicted to them in a dream and eight per cent have visited a faith healer. I believe that the figures for America are even higher than these from the UK.

Today many people are seeking answers to their spiritual questions and turning to people like myself for answers. To conclude, here are a few of the most frequently asked that are most often sent to my columns with my answers based upon my experience of mediumship and clairvoyance. I may yet be wrong in many of my conclusions but I believe that we're beginning at least to ask the right questions.

Is everybody psychic?

There are many people who are openly antagonistic to people who claim to be psychic. Many of these narrow minded individuals would deny the evidence no matter how overwhelmingly in favour of the existence of ESP. In this vendetta the scientists and the fundamentalist Christians share a common goal in discrediting the claims of psychics for, if what we say is true, then their treasured beliefs will be shaken to the very foundations. A person who is really in search of the truth is not upset if Truth turns out to be different from their preconceptions.

Those who deny their psychic powers suppress them but that's not to say that these unused gifts are not still latent within them. I believe that everyone has **latent** psychic powers and may even have latent powers of materialisation. With the growing acceptance of psychic powers the phenomena will continue to grow stronger. Many people believe that we are entering a new age of expanded consciousness and will soon witness incredible things in the years to come.

Can I increase my latent powers?

I have found that I can train most open-minded people to develop ESP but only a few are able to develop their mediumistic skills. Psychic development works best within a group or a Spiritualist circle. In this environment there is much more energy to work with and the support of everyone around you will give you the confidence to advance. Also the collective power of a group of people working together is greater than the sum total of each person's energy. A list of techniques and organisations can be found in my previous book *The Psychic Handbook* (Vermilion)

Are psychic powers and spirituality related?

Unfortunately all types of people can be psychic. Rasputin for example had the power to hypnotise people from a distance yet was a man of evil intent, the Fox sisters were Spiritualism's most important mediums yet they were unintelligent country girls and Helen Duncan was an incredible materialisation medium yet her manner was coarse and sometimes vulgar. Psychic powers may spontaneously occur in people who have attained a high degree of spiritual unfoldment but powers are not necessarily proof of good character. For example, if someone has a beautiful voice that can move people to tears it doesn't necessarily mean that they are a beautiful person.

Can we change the future?

Our destiny is decided by our karma. Fortunately we can get rid of bad karma by good inner and outer behaviour. The best way to change the future for the better is to change ourselves. The power of free will can be directed outwardly into the world to bring us worldly things but becomes most effective when we direct it at ourselves to bring about an inner transformation. This is the highest way to change our destiny. Therefore, the objective of fortune telling should be to give the sitter the guidance so that they can find spiritual solutions to their material worries. In this way even a negative destiny can be reversed. In short it's not about telling the future; it's about changing the future.

Do animals have psychic powers?

Animals with psychic powers would have a greater chance of survival than those without them. Telepathy would be useful to give warnings to the herd about predators, clairvoyance would help an animal find its way or locate the whereabouts of water and precognition would help an animal anticipate an attack. A sensitivity to vibration would help animals to 'smell death' in places that are dangerous or know when a place is safe. And some animals stroke their fellow creatures when they're ill- indicating perhaps a desire to heal.

But there's a higher function of psychic powers that only humans have. Just as Sai Baba has the power to materialise objects, appear in two places at once and perform the impossible so too these powers are within the reach of every human being. Once we awaken the higher spiritual forces reality itself changes and we can perform acts that the materialist would consider impossible. It is only in the human form that we can attain this state of being.

What happens after death?

At brain death we shed the physical body as we would a suit of clothes and progress to the spirit world in our astral body. This is a temporary form and is made of a material that is on a higher vibration to gross matter. As we progress we shed this etheric sheath and enter into the realms of pure spirit which is indescribable in earthly terms, the closest metaphor for this state is that it is a 'world of light'.

At the point of death some people are aware of the material world but most fall into the 'tunnel of light' that is often described by people who have come back from the brink of death. NDE cases usually describe reaching a demarcation point, (sometimes symbolised by a fence, pearly gates or a stairway) -cross this threshold and there's no returning to the physical body. We are then greeted by those we love who have gone before us and we become aware of God who appears to us in the form we are most familiar with. An atheist or Buddhist may experience God as a light, a Hindu may see Krishna, a Moslem may see Mohammed or the light of Allah and a Christian may see the form of Jesus.

Does the human personality survive death?

Mediumship indicates that the personality, with all its quirks, idiosyncrasies and memories, survives death. It is reassuring to know that the dead we love continue in the next word. They remain just as we knew them but minus their bodily aliments.

But this is not the final spiritual goal- for what is the personality? Who are you? The personality is only the outer trappings of something greater, it is not your quintessence. The goal of human life is to realise our divinity, to directly merge with the God within us. A Buddhist will tell you that the personality and the self are illusions. The real you is the consciousness within which is never born into either in the material world or the heavenly world. The best place to realise this inner divinity is here on Earth and the spirit planes a just a sojourn between lives.

Will I meet the people I dislike such as my ex-marital partner in the next world?

Like attracts like. In the spirit world you will come together with those you love most and who you are bound to by a higher 'Overself'. The people who have troubled you in life will go their own way. However when the purpose of your life is revealed to you then you may see that the negative people were sent to test you for a specific reason. Despite the pain they've caused, you may understand that they are not evildoers but sent so that you may spiritually flower. God gives his hardest tests to his most advanced pupils.

Do animals survive death?

As I see it there are two sorts of animals: those that have an individual consciousness and those that are part of a group consciousness. Pets, for example, develop a greater sense of identity because of their contact with humans. Although most of their behaviour is instinctive they also appear to gain a certain degree of self-awareness. They may have also experienced love. I believe that these influences help form an individual soul that retains its sense of identity after death. I am reminded of one lady who came for a mediumistic consultation: "Don't tell me anything about the humans over there" she said "I only want to know about my cats." I was able to give her the names of all eight of her cats and character traits that each had. Although I believe I had her 'dead' father helping me it proved to me that some animals survive death and, like us, retain their characteristics beyond the grave.

I also believe, although I have no empirical proof of this, that most animals merge into the collective consciousness of their species after death.

How do you square the idea of reincarnation with the Spiritualist evidence for an afterlife?

You have read a number of stories in this book that suggest that reincarnation is a fact and yet have also read of cases that suggest that there is an afterlife. Although these two ideas may seen diametrically opposed I believe that both beliefs can be brought together as one. The Hindus believe that everyone has an eternal soul called the *Jiva*. It has never been born and can exist forever- a concept similar to the Spiritualist fourth principle that says: 'The continuous existence of the human soul'. The *Jiva's* nature is innately pure but by evil deeds it has become clothed in ignorance. After death the *Jiva* leaves the material body and goes to the solar regions of which there are spheres upon spheres. (This corresponds with the 'many mansions' of Christianity, the spheres of the afterlife as described by Spiritualists or the *Bardos* of the Tibetan Buddhists)

The earth is the world sphere in which there are moons, suns and stars but beyond this is the Lunar sphere and beyond this is the sphere of lightning. In this high realm the *Jiva* is taken to the highest heaven called the *Brahmaloka* where it can live for eternity and never be born or die again. Only the perfected souls who have given up all desires can live in this exalted state. This differs somewhat from the Spiritualist precept that there is 'Eternal progress open to every human soul' which suggests that there is no final goal to existence.

The less high souls may enter the lunar sphere as an angelic being where it may enjoy a prolonged period of happiness but this last only for as long as the effect of its good deeds endures. Once this good karma is exhausted it descends again into the earth sphere and takes a new human birth. The person in the spirit world dies and is reborn in human form. Also, in these realms there is a hierarchy of beings which corresponds with the third spiritualist principle of there being a 'Ministry of Angels'. Furthermore the fact that our sojourn in the spirit world is dictated by our karma agrees with the Spiritualist belief that we must take 'personal responsibility' for our destiny.

In short, I believe that our stay in the Afterlife worlds is only temporary. Whilst in these ethereal worlds we do not accumulate either good or bad karma. However our period in the afterlife is fuelled by the karma accumulated on earth prior to our death. When the soul's good Karma is worked out, then the remaining Karma begins to take effect, and the soul comes down to earth to become a human again. If the person continues to do spiritual work and purifies himself then they may finally go to Brahmaloka and need come back no more.

Can animals take human birth?

Metempsychosis is a theory dating from before the ancient Greeks that says that every living thing reincarnates. In the course of time the animal becomes man. It is interesting to note that the human population is increasing while the animal population is decreasing. Perhaps these animal souls are all becoming human? The Tibetan Buddhists emphasise how important and rare it is to have a 'precious human birth'- we live for aeons of time in animal form and a human birth, with its chance to attain enlightenment, is a tremendous opportunity. I personally find it fascinating to watch people's behaviour and observe their animal characteristics. Some people pout like fish, slink like cats or charge ahead like bulls. How many people do you know that chatter like birds, eat like pigs or behave like rats?

Can aliens take human birth?

I've met 'mediums' who have spoken with the squeaky voice of an alien and met several mixed-up people who claim to be 'abductees'. So far I'm completely unconvinced by what I've seen and heard although I believe that it's inevitable, given the size of the universe, that there is life on other planets. I cannot answer this question with any authority however Sai Baba was asked this same question and said that alien life reincarnates in its own star system and have their own afterlife worlds.

Will I always find the people I love?

People who love each other share their karma. I believe that there exists a group soul of which our individual selves are emanations. Soul mates can include parents, family, children and friends as well as lovers and partners. Those that love each other will be drawn together in the afterlife and in future earthly lives.

Who are the spirit guides?

It is possible that the spirit guides may be aspects of our own psychology that have become disassociated from the personality and taken on a life of their own. They could also be what the Tibetans call *Tulpas* which are genielike beings created by the concentrated power of thought. However my own conclusion is that the spirit guides are real beings that come to help us. I come to this verdict because my own spirit guides have supplied me with evidence of their reality via the mouthpiece of other mediums. All of us have a spirit guide which some call the guardian angel.

Is there a Hell?

When Christianity spread throughout Europe it supplant the ancient pagan gods and built its churches upon their most sacred sites. Everything associated with these old religions was branded as evil. For example, traditionally Pan was the cloven footed god of fertility who brought happiness and jollity. To supplant him the Christians portrayed him as the devil and lord of Hell.

There is no inescapable Hell as such but Spiritualists believe that the afterlife consists of many spheres of existence some of which are 'lower' planes. All souls are innately divine but can become corrupted by their evil deeds. The heaviness of their vibration makes them sink like a stone to the lower spheres. Here they are guided by wise souls to reform their ways and, in time, given another chance at life- possibly in animal form.

It is interesting to note how close Spiritualist ideas are to the Hindu beliefs. In the Vedas there is no mention of hell but in the Puranas (the later books) these regions are described in detail. Here the bad karma is worked out through pain and suffering but mercifully the offender is finally given another chance at life on earth.

What is the reason for suffering?
Joy lead to complacency and often sorrow is our greatest teacher. Both come to us because of the karma generated by our actions. However, the middle way leads to realisation of our divinity and the release from suffering as beautifully expressed by the poet William Blake: "Man was made for joy and woe, And when this we rightly know, Safely through the world we go."

What is the purpose of life?
To realise that we are One.

ABOUT THE AUTHOR

Craig Hamilton-Parker is a British author, television personality and professional psychic medium. He is best known for his TV shows *Our Psychic Family*, *The Spirit of Diana* and *Nightmares Decoded*. On television he usually works with his wife Jane Hamilton-Parker who is also a psychic medium. Their work was showcased in a three part documentary on the BBC called *Mediums Talking to the Dead*.

They now have TV shows in the USA and spend a lot of time demonstrating mediumship around the world.

Born in Southampton UK, Craig was convinced at an early age that he was mediumistic. He became a well known as a platform medium within Spiritualism and in 1994 left his job as advertising executive to become the resident psychic on Channel 4 television's *The Big Breakfast* making predictions for upcoming news stories. He wrote a regular psychic advice column for *The Scottish Daily Record* and regular features for *The Daily Mail*, *Sunday Mirror* and *The People*.

His first book about the psychic genre was published in 1995 and are now find a world audience and are published in many languages.

You can find out more and join Craig & Jane's work and Spiritual Foundation at their website: **psychics.co.uk**

PUBLISHED BOOKS

Hamilton-Parker, Craig & Jane (1995) *The Psychic Workbook* Random House ISBN 0-09-179086-7 (Languages: English, Chinese)

Hamilton-Parker, Craig (1996) *Your Psychic Powers* Hodder & Stoughton ISBN 0-340-67417-2 (Languages: English)

Hamilton-Parker, Craig (1999) *Timeless Wisdom of the Tibetans* Hodder & Stoughton ISBN 0-340-70483-7 (Languages: English)

Hamilton-Parker, Craig (1999) *The Psychic Casebook* Blandford/Sterling ISBN 0-7137-2755-1 (Languages: English, Turkish)

Hamilton-Parker, Craig (1999) *The Hidden Meaning of Dreams* Sterling imprint Barnes & Noble ISBN 0-8069-7773-6 (Languages: English, Spanish, Portuguese, Russian, Israeli, Greek Icelandic.)

Hamilton-Parker, Craig (2000) *The Intuition Pack* Godfield Books ISBN 1-84181-007-X

Hamilton-Parker, Craig (2000) *Remembering Your Dreams* Sterling imprint Barnes & Noble ISBN 0-8069-4343-2

Hamilton-Parker, Craig (2000) *Unlock Your Secret Dreams* Sterling imprint Barnes & Noble ISBN 1-4027-0316-3

Hamilton-Parker, Craig (2002) *Fantasy Dreaming* Sterling imprint Barnes & Noble ISBN 0-8069-5478-7

Hamilton-Parker, Craig (2003) *Protecting the Soul* Sterling imprint Barnes & Noble ISBN 0-8069-8719-7

Hamilton-Parker, Craig (2004) *Psychic Dreaming* Sterling imprint Barnes & Noble ISBN 1-4027-0474-7

Hamilton-Parker, Craig (2005) *Opening to the Other Side* Sterling imprint Barnes & Noble ISBN 1-4027-1346-0

Hamilton-Parker, Craig (2010) *What To Do When You Are Dead* Sterling imprint Barnes & Noble ISBN 978-1-4027-7660-1 (Languages: English, Dutch, Portuguese)

YOU MAY ALSO ENJOY CRAIG'S MEDITATION CD

Opening to Inner Light

Craig Hamilton-Parker
psychics.co.uk

Opening to Inner Light is a **CD narrated by Craig Hamilton-Parker that is designed to take you into meditation and awaken the chakras, open the aura and directly connect you to the spirit world.**

This CD is set to beautiful music and is used by psychics and mediums to enhance their powers and is also a powerful tool for inner transformation that can be used by everyone. *Opening to Inner Light* will bring you deep peace and a feeling of being connected to the Universe.

Available from: psychics.co.uk

Printed in Great Britain
by Amazon.co.uk, Ltd.,
Marston Gate.